Managing Archaeological Collections in Middle Eastern Countries

A Good Practice Guide

Dianne Fitzpatrick

Archaeopress Archaeology

ARCHAEOPRESS PUBLISHING LTD
SUMMERTOWN PAVILION
18-24 MIDDLE WAY
OXFORD OX2 7LG

www.archaeopress.com

ISBN 978 1 78491 488 2
ISBN 978 1 78491 489 9 (e-Pdf)

© Archaeopress and D Fitzpatrick 2016

All rights reserved. No part of this book may be reproduced, or transmitted, in any form or by any means, electronic, mechanical, photocopying or otherwise, without the prior written permission of the copyright owners.

This book is available direct from Archaeopress or from our website www.archaeopress.com

Contents

Aims and Objectives 1
   Artefacts Recovered from Archaeological Excavation and Fieldwork 1
   Records and Documents 1
   Background 3
      Pre-Excavation Project Design 4
      Excavation 6
      Post-Excavation 8
   Preservation and Re-Use 9

Archaeological Collections Management Practice 13
   What is Archaeological Collections Management Practice? 13
   Planning for the Creation of Collections 13
      Governance 13
   Collections Management Strategies 15
      Phases of Archaeological Process 16
      Written or Formal Policies 17
   Conserving and Caring for Archaeological Collections 17
      Specialised Environmental Storage 17

Archaeological Collections Management 19
      Governance and Principles 19
      Current Management, Strategies and Approaches 22
   Artefacts in Archaeologial Collections 23
      Documentation System and Digital Archive 24
      Storage Provision and Future Expansion Needs 24
      Levels of Use of the Collections 25
   Archaeological Collections Management Practices in Middle Eastern Countries 27
      Forward Planning 27

Recording Archaeological Collections 28
   Management System for Collecting, Processing, Analysing and Curating 28
      General Requirements 28
      Management Structure 29
      Collections Management Responsibilities 29
      Regulatory Responsibilities 30
      Management Planning and System Review 30
      Documentation 30
      General 31
      Operational Procedures 31
      Control of Documents 31
      Control of Records 33
      Resource Management 33
      Provision of Resources 33

- Human Resources 34
- Infrastructure 34
- Artefact Types and Characteristics 34
  - Collections Assessment 35
  - Estimation of Collections Scope and Size for New Sites 35
  - Collections Scope and Size for Existing Sites 35
  - Description of Collections 35
  - Storage Crates, Boxes, Shelving Facilities 36
  - Condition of Archaeological Collections 36
  - Conservation and Preservation 36
  - Storage Facilities 36
  - Buildings: Shelters, Laboratories, Storage, Site Museum 37
  - Collections Management 37
  - Collections Management Objectives 37
  - Collections Management Policies 37
  - Field Collection 37
  - Salvage Excavation 37
  - Field Conservation And Preservation 38
  - Registration 38
  - Laboratory Sampling and Management 38
  - Laboratory Conservation 39
  - Discard 39
  - Cataloguing 39
  - Labelling 39
  - Packing 39
  - Storage Environment 39
  - Conservation and Preservation 40
  - Inventory 40
- Records and Data Management Systems 40
  - Data Storage and Retrieval System 41
  - Paper Archive 41
  - Publications 41
  - Electronic, Film and Photographic Archives 41
  - Access and Use of Collections 41

Short-Term: Registration, Analysis And Access 43
- The Collections Management System 43
  - Policies and Procedures 43
  - Loans 44
  - Researcher Access 44
  - Destructive Analysis 44
  - Legal 44
  - Inventory Management 44
  - Annual Inventory of Collections 44
  - Object Locations 45
  - Collections Annual Report 45

　　　　Collections Significance Criteria 45
　　　　Security and Succession Planning 45
　　　　Emergency Planning/Disaster Response 45
　　　　Threats to Archaeological Collections 46
　　　　Threats to Documentary Archive 46
　　Role of Registrars 46
　　Role of Conservators 47
　　Role of Archaeological Specialists 47
　　Assessing Significance 48
　　Access to On-Site Collections 50

Long-Term: Archaeological Collections Storage 51
　　Standard for Storing and Curating On-Site Archaeological Collections 51
　　　　International Charters and Conventions 51
　　　　United Nations Educational and Scientific Organisation (UNESCO) 51
　　　　International Centre for the Study of the Preservation and Restoration of Cultural
　　　　Property (ICCROM) 53
　　　　International Council on Monuments and Sites (ICOMOS) 53
　　　　International Council of Museums (ICOM) 55
　　　　Archaeological Site Management and Conservation 56
　　Estimating Storage Provision and Future Expansion Needs 56
　　On-Site Storage Facilities for Archaeological Collections 58
　　Funding 59
　　Directorates and Museums 60
　　Accessing Archaeological Collections in Museums, On-Site and Remotely 61

Implementing Archaeological Collections Management Strategies 63
　　Recommendations for Governments 63
　　Recommendations for Funding Bodies 64
　　Recommendations for Archaeologists 64

Summary 66
　　Reasons for Managing Archaeological Collections 66
　　Code for Managing Archaeological Collections Into the Future 66

Glossary 69

Bibliography 71

Appendix 1: Field Study: Syria and Turkey 85

Appendix 2: Survey: Archaeologists, Conservators and Curators 105

List of Figures

Figure 1: Phases of English Heritage (MoRPHE) model 7
Figure 2: Conservation considerations 11
Figure 3: Preparation for long-term storage... 12
Figure 4: Archaeological collections management system... 14
Figure 5: Recommendations for post-examination artefact treatment and storage 18
Figure 6 International minimum standards for documenting archaeological collections 20
Figure 7: Research categories and participating specialists 2003-2012 26
Figure 8: Tell Ta'yinat 'object' triage process.. 47
Figure 9: Most to least 'useful' rating 49
Figure 10: ICOM/CIDOC Standards and Guidelines 56
Figure 11: On-site storage space projection 57
Figure 12: Elements of an archaeological collections management plan................................... 68

Figure 1.1 Syrian Arab Republic governance structure... 85
Figure 1.2 Organisational structure of Jebel Khalid in 2010 86
Figure 1.3 Breakdown of human resources, work hours and quantities excavated 87
Figure 1.4 Inventoried (registered) objects from Area A Trench 502 87
Figure 1.5 Organisational structure of Tell Ahmar in 2010 88
Figure 1.6 Breakdown of human resources, work hours and quantities excavated in 2010 89
Figure 1.7 Total hours worked to re-pack TAH archaeological collections................................. 89
Figure 1.8 Turkish government central organisation 90
Figure 1.9 Turkish government provincial organization 91
Figure 1.10 Organisational structure of Çatalhöyük in 2010 92
Figure 1.11 Collecting strategy at Çatalhöyük 93
Figure 1.12 Overview of research categories and participating specialists from 2003 to 2012 94
Figure 1.13 Çatalhöyük artefact categories and crate quantities 95
Figure 1.14 Quantities of core artefact categories and percentage of collection....................... 96
Figure 1.15 Çatalhöyük storage depot measurements and crate capacities 96
Figure 1.16 Estimation of capacity 96
Figure 1.17 Çatalhöyük storage depot cost 96
Figure 1.18 Organisational structure of Tell Ta'yinat in 2012 97
Figure 1.19 Tell Ta'yinat 'Triage' system 98
Figure 1.20 Policies, processes and procedures in the TAP Field Manual 99
Figure 1.21 Total storage expressed as crates 99
Figure 1.22 TAP annual crate accumulation 100
Figure 1.23 Tell Ta'yinat storage depot measurements and crate capacities 100
Figure 1.24 Estimation of capacity 100
Figure 1.25 Number of artefacts accessioned 2006 to 2011... 100
Figure 1.26 Organisational structure of Antiochia ad Cragum in 2013..................................... 101
Figure 1.27 Antiochia ad Cragum artefact categories and quantities....................................... 102
Figure 1.28 Configuration of metal shelving units.. 103
Figure 1.29 Crate accumulations 2009 to 2012 104

Figure 2.1: Site types directed by survey participants. 105
Figure 2.2: Key groups and survey categories. 105
Figure 2.3: Countries in which archaeologists were working or had worked. 106
Figure 2.4: Duration of archaeological projects. 106
Figure 2.5: Duration of project directorships. 106
Figure 2.6: Relationships of archaeological project stakeholders. 106
Figure 2.7: Duration of funding for archaeological projects. 106
Figure 2.8: Specifications for objectives and resources are included in project designs. 106
Figure 2.9: Specifications for aims and costs are included in project designs. 107
Figure 2.10: Specifications for strategies and resources are included in project designs. 107
Figure 2.11: Specifications for assignations are included in project designs. 107
Figure 2.12: Specifications for archive recipients are included in project designs. 107
Figure 2.13: Annual updates of project designs are provided. 107
Figure 2.14: IT systems are used for pre-excavation management. 107
Figure 2.15: IT systems are used for on-site management. 108
Figure 2.16: IT systems are used for post-excavation management. 108
Figure 2.17: Types of programs and software used throughout project phases. 108
Figure 2.18: Specialists identify work needing to be carried out on-site. 108
Figure 2.19: Timetables and budgets allow for visits by conservators and specialists. 108
Figure 2.20: Projects arrange long-term care with museums in the planning stage. 108
Figure 2.21: Projects budget for long-term care of non-artefactual material. 108
Figure 2.22: Projects provide written training manuals for students and/or volunteers. 109
Figure 2.23: Archaeologists are in favour of keeping a collection in perpetuity. 109
Figure 2.24: Projects specify an artefact collecting policy. 109
Figure 2.25: Projects specify an artefact sampling policy. 109
Figure 2.26: Projects specify an artefact discard policy. 109
Figure 2.27: Projects specify a sampling strategy for redundant objects. 109
Figure 2.28: Archaeologists' rating of significance criteria in order of most to least useful. 109
Figure 2.29: Projects brief relevant consultants on data collection policies. 110
Figure 2.30: Projects explain on-site procedures to excavators. 110
Figure 2.31: Projects undertake individual training. 110
Figure 2.32: Projects have a system for detecting errors made during fieldwork. 110
Figure 2.33: Documents and records comprising the primary data archive. 110
Figure 2.34: Numbers of inventoried (registered) objects per season. 110
Figure 2.35: Percentage of inventoried objects accessioned by museums. 111
Figure 2.36: Approximate numbers of objects requiring conservation. 111
Figure 2.37: Written notification of conservation treatments is provided. 111
Figure 2.38: Written notification of further conservation work required is provided. 111
Figure 2.39: Approximate (kg) amount of excavated material each season. 111
Figure 2.40: Archaeological projects have storage facilities on-site or nearby. 111
Figure 2.41: Duration of adequacy and availability of storage space. 111
Figure 2.42: Total space (m3) occupied by artefacts and collections. 112
Figure 2.43: Archaeologists access archaeological collections for research. 112

Figure 2.44: Artefacts and collections are easily accessible. 112
Figure 2.45: Artefacts and collections are in good condition. 112
Figure 2.46: Artefacts and collections have an accompanying archive. 112
Figure 2.47: Countries in which conservators worked or had worked. 112
Figure 2.48: Conservators' rating of significance criteria in order of most to least useful. 113
Figure 2.49: Conservators give advice about conservation interventions performed. 113
Figure 2.50: Conservators give advice for long-term care of objects/collections. 113
Figure 2.51: Conservators are satisfied with on-site resources. 113
Figure 2.52: Conservators are trained in archaeological excavation techniques. 113
Figure 2.53: Conservators believe archaeologists have a good understanding of conservation. 113
Figure 2.54: Countries in which curators worked or had worked. 114
Figure 2.55: Curators' rating of significance criteria in order of most to least useful. 114
Figure 2.56: Archaeological collections are held in museums/repositories. 114
Figure 2.57: Museums/repositories have written guidelines for packing artefacts and collections. 114
Figure 2.58: Museums/repositories specify expectations upon delivery of artefacts/collections. 114
Figure 2.59: Museums/repositories request objects in a stabilised and/or conserved condition. 114
Figure 2.60: Museums/repositories receive advice detailing conservation treatments needed. .. 115
Figure 2.61: Museums/repositories have a curation agreement. 115
Figure 2.62: Museums/repositories receive advice detailing long-term plans for collections. ... 115
Figure 2.63: Museums/repositories are involved in the excavation process. 115
Figure 2.64: Museums/repositories specify ownership of artefacts/collections. 115

Acknowledgements

The author would like to express her most sincere thanks to all those who supported the doctoral study.

Special thanks must go to Dr. Andrew Jamieson and Dr. Brent Davis from the Classics and Archaeology Program at the University of Melbourne, Australia and to the case study site directors who generously provided full access to their sites.

In order of site visits they are:

Dr Heather Jackson, University of Melbourne, Australia
Professor Graeme Clarke, Australian National University, Australia
Professor Guy Bunnens, University of Liege, Belgium
Dr Arlette Bunnens, University of Liege, Belgium
Professor Ian Hodder, Stanford University, United States of America
Professor Timothy Harrison, University of Toronto, Canada
Professor Michael Hoff, University of Nebraska-Lincoln, United States of America

Additional people who deserve thanks include the many archaeologists, conservators and curators working, or who had worked, in Afghanistan, Australia, Cyprus, Egypt, Greece, Iran, Israel, Jordan, Lebanon, Sicily, Syria, Turkey, the United Arab Emirates, the United Kingdom, and the United States of America, who participated in the survey but who elected to remain anonymous.

Their contributions to the study provided invaluable insight into current archaeological collections management practice in the Middle East.

Aims and Objectives

Artefacts Recovered from Archaeological Excavation and Fieldwork

One of the outcomes of conducting archaeological survey and/or excavation or other study is the recovery of large quantities of archaeological material each year from sites. In the Middle East recovered artefacts fall into several categories. An artefact could be somewhat unique or rarer compared to all others so that it is registered with a special catalogue number, and commonly called a 'special find.' It may have historic, aesthetic, scientific or social value and is considered to be a 'value' of the site from where it was recovered. In many countries very small quantities of unique or characteristically diagnostic objects are accessioned by museums with the remaining artefacts kept in storage depots at archaeological sites. Diagnostic artefacts such as vessel rims, pot handles or bone elements are another category which may provide archaeologists with statistical data for analyses. Bulk and non-diagnostic artefacts are other categories, for instance soil samples, which may provide pollen samples or other data suitable for archaeometric testing or scientific analyses. In many cases these are stored on-site. It is a legal requirement in some countries that at the end of each excavation season, a selection of registered artefacts is accessioned into a regional or national museum, while in other countries all registered artefacts are accessioned by museums or stored in governmental depots. As much legislation in many countries does not contain specifics for how on-site archaeological collections should be managed in the short and long-term a need exists for sustainable means for preserving and caring for artefacts which are either put into storage or discarded.

Records and Documents

In addition to recovering quantities of physical artefacts another outcome of archaeological fieldwork is the production of records and documents which constitute a primary project archive. According to archaeologists who work or have worked in the Middle East, their project archive consists of paper and/or digital context records; maps, plans, sections; photographic records; datasets for artefacts and samples; finds records, registers, catalogues, inventories; field notebooks and diaries; computer discs and print-outs; survey and GIS (Global Information System) records; and conservation, sample, skeleton and x-ray records. Hence artefacts, or material remains that are excavated or removed during a survey, excavation or other study of a prehistoric or historic resource, and the associated records that are prepared or assembled in connection with the survey, excavation or other study represent 'archaeological collections'. Managing and caring for archaeological collections with concern for their long-term physical well-being and safety is a specific activity known as 'archaeological collections management practice.' On-site archaeological collections management practice is governed by site policies and procedures. Conveying the site policy and conducting the archaeological collections management procedures is in many cases performed by a site registrar or conservator. Documenting the organisational and operational activities which includes issues of conservation, access and use and inventory may be carried out by a site registrar or collections management team.[1]

Instigating long-term measures for care and preservation of on-site archaeological collections is not a traditional practice amongst all archaeological project directors. Consequently, vast amounts of archaeological material stored at sites in the Middle East are now at risk of deterioration and destruction. Increasingly, regional governments and international cultural heritage bodies are seeking ways to better mitigate risks that threaten archaeological sites and thus the collections stored there. Therefore, the aim of this monograph entitled, *Managing Archaeological Collections in Middle Eastern Countries: A Good Practice Guide* is to propose sustainable measures that seek to assist invested stakeholders in managing artefact collections. The greatest area of concern for archaeological project directors, conservators and curators is the lack of formal policies for managing archaeological collections (Appendix 1 Field study: Syria and Turkey; Appendix 2 Survey: Archaeologists, Conservators and Curators).[2] Hence this *Good Practice Guide* is intended to assist:

- Governmental bodies which permit international archaeological projects to conduct survey or excavation projects (see recommendation 63).
- Institutional and private funding bodies that grant monies for conducting archaeological research and fieldwork (see recommendation 64).
- Archaeological project directors who conduct archaeological surveys, or excavations or other studies in the Middle East (see recommendation 64).

---

[1] US National Park Service 2015. Glossary Website: http://.nps.gov/archeology/collections/glossary.htm (10/09/2015).

[2] Fitzpatrick 2015. *Collections at Risk: An examination of archaeological collections management practice in the Near East*. PhD diss., University of Melbourne. The doctoral research was conducted at the Classics and Archaeology Program at the University of Melbourne 2009-2015. The study involved a literature review of cultural heritage legislation and models for managing archaeological collections, a survey of archaeologists, conservators and curators and field study at archaeological sites in Syria and Turkey 2010-2013. The case studies were Jebel Khalid, Syria, a Hellenistic site (University of Melbourne; Australian National University); Tell Ahmar, Syria, a Neo-Assyrian site (Liege University); Çatalhöyük, Turkey, a Neolithic site (Stanford University); Tell Ta'yinat, Turkey, a Bronze Age/Iron Age site (University of Toronto); and Antiochia ad Cragum, Turkey, a Roman site (University of Nebraska-Lincoln). The author wishes to thank the project directors for their permission to conduct this study and to the collections management staff for their help during the field seasons. The survey involved archaeologists, conservators and curators who currently work or had worked in Afghanistan, Cyprus, Egypt, Greece, Iran, Israel, Jordan, Lebanon, Sicily, Syria, Turkey, and the United Arab Emirates.

Background

Artefact classes and typologies are culturally diverse objects or collections of objects made or crafted by people inhabiting geographic landscapes throughout the pre-historic and historic periods. A breakdown of survey responses from current archaeological project directors indicates that 47% of sites are Bronze Age/Iron Age; 31% are Pre-Classical/Classical; 10% are Neolithic; 6% are Chalcolithic; 3% are Islamic and 3% are Palaeolithic.[3] Analysis and interpretation of physical and material characteristics by archaeological specialists permit a host of narratives to be constructed about artefacts and collections that provide knowledge about their historic, aesthetic, scientific or social values. According to models for assessing cultural heritage significance, charters and other doctrinal texts (CIDOC 1995; Council of Europe 1992; Demas 2003: 38-46 *Annotated Bibliography III*; ICAHM 2010; 2008; ICCROM 2011; 1995; ICCROM-UNESCO n.d; ICOM 1995; ICOMOS 2011a-d; 2005; 2002; 1999a-d; 1990; 1964; ICOMOS Committee for Documentation of Cultural Heritage 2015; ICOMOS Australia 2014; 2013; 2004 and 1999; Russell and Winkworth 2009:10; UNESCO 2008; 1972a; 1972b; 1956), the cultural heritage values imbued in artefacts contribute to interpreting the place from where they were recovered and should be assessed using these set criteria. Four comparative modifiers further help evaluate the degree of significance relative to an artefact or collections' provenance, rarity, condition or interpretive capacity.

An artefact is deemed to be of scientific significance if researchers have an active interest in studying it now or in the future. Its characteristics, the nature and scope of its contribution or value for science now or in the future also make it significant. However, the nature of this method of assessment is not particularly helpful for managing vast numbers of research collections created by the archaeological process(es). Site management and conservation plans aim to preserve archaeological sites but do not include strategies for managing scientific research data and artefact collections. Current standards and guidelines do not adequately take into account the decisions that are made at the completion of a project that has produced archival data and physical objects, both of which require long-term management and preservation for future generations. Adding to the problem is that much of the cultural heritage legislation in the Middle East lacks definition and does not contain policy for short and long-term management of archaeological collections.

---

[3] The average duration for archaeological research projects in the Middle East is 23.5 years. Some projects have been running discontinuously for more than a century. The duration of an archaeological 'contract' or 'salvage' project can as brief as four weeks. As many artefacts are gathered as is possible within the given timeframe and may be stored in a directorate depot. Little or no research is conducted on these artefacts. They are eventually discarded.

One of the legacies inherited by countries in the Middle East is that current laws and regulations are founded on the 1922 British and French Mandates for Lebanon and Syria. Consequently, some administrative systems continue to exist that are out-of-date and act as knowledge barriers. Although amendments have been made since that period which are more focused on conservation and sustainability, many laws fail to specify accepted international standard practice for managing archaeological artefacts and collections. A review of cultural heritage legislation reveals that frameworks which underpin current practice were founded in the Ottoman period when regional museums were satellite outposts linked to national museums.[4] Although the system was modified during the Mandate period it was retained by the English and French until those countries gained independence in the 1940s. Because of those long-established systems, many governments today are disadvantaged. Added to this is the lack of resources which impedes growth of opportunities for professional development, education and training. On-site archaeological collections management practice may involve some or all of these activities:

- Cataloguing
- Classification and conservation systems for collections
- Collections management systems
- Handling and packing
- Inventory and security
- Object cleaning and conservation
- Object identification
- Pest management and housekeeping
- Quantifying collections
- Registering artefacts
- Significance criteria
- Writing an archaeological collections management plan
- Accessioning
- Installing an exhibition
- Preparing texts for exhibits
- Selecting objects for exhibition

Pre-Excavation Project Design

Operational projects require laboratories, work areas and storage facilities to process artefacts, although on-site storage is required in many countries after a project has been completed on an ongoing and indefinite basis. At a systematic level when an artefact is recovered, it is assessed on the basis of whether it is relevant to the research questions being asked. The condition or preservation quality of an artefact is also considered. It is influenced by the availability of

---

[4] Egypt, Israel, Jordan, Syria and Turkey.

financial resources, time and space. After artefacts are quantified an indication is gained as to whether it is possible to answer the research questions based on the characteristics and categories of artefacts. These processes occur as part of the on-site fieldwork and excavation process. Further analysis and interpretation of artefacts is conducted by category specialists, and scientific testing may be carried out at their expert discretion if necessary. Data that produce typological and chronological or taxonomic classifications are analysed, which may include details of condition and wear patterns, chronology and typology based on shape, spatial distribution and attribution to a culture. Cultural significance in its many forms may be determined as a result. These results are disseminated to wider audiences through reports, articles, books, theses and other media. On average more than 1 tonne of archaeological material is excavated at each archaeological site in the Middle East each season (Appendix 2). Consolidating an archaeological project takes considerable effort and time, and also requires a high level of planning. International guidelines specify that procedures applicable to collecting, processing and storing artefacts must all correspond to the project design.[5]

For instance, 93% of archaeologists specify the objectives of the project and resources necessary in their project designs, whereas 88% specify the phase-related aims and the costs. 96% percent specify the strategies and resources appropriate to the fieldwork phase and 95% specify the assignations of the core team and specialists. 83% specify the museum or other body that will receive the eventual project archive, whereas 88% update this information each year. 89% estimate what the physical nature, including condition, of their archaeological collections will be each season, whereas all participants indicated that their data collection methods clearly describe how the data will fulfil the aims of their project. 93% indicated that the potential character of their data assists in formulating the academic objectives of their project, whereas a very high percentage of archaeologists understand what types of artefacts will be recovered, as well as the physical nature of the archaeological collections each season. 90% used computer/IT systems in the pre-excavation planning phase, whereas 80% use them on-site during the excavation operational phase. A variety of off-the-shelf and purpose-made computer programs and software types are used in the planning pre-excavation, excavation and post-excavation phases. These include:

- Specialised software
- Access database
- Excel
- Filemaker Pro
- Photoshop; Illustrator

---

[5] Willems and Brandt 2004, 148,

- Relational databases
- Word
- Other

In the planning phase of their projects 93% of archaeologists involve and consult with specialists about the type of work needed to be done on-site and how it should be conducted. Many specialists conduct analytical work on-site during the excavation season, however the duration of their time on-site varies. Some 80% of archaeologists plan ahead in their timetables and budgets for visits by conservators and other specialists although 53% are in favour of keeping a collection in its entirety in perpetuity, whereas 47% are in favour of discarding the material.[6] Less than half of archaeologists plan ahead with national or local museums for the long-term care of accessioned artefacts or collections, and less than half budget for long-term care of on-site collections. More than half of archaeologists provide written policy manuals, which include references on initial sorting and classification followed by a second stage of sorting and classification once artefacts are washed and processed before specialist analyses occurs. 68% of project designs specify the aims and objectives of an artefact collections policy, whereas 60% specify the aims and objectives of a sampling policy. Less than half specify the aims and objectives of a discard policy, whereas one-third specify the aims and objectives of a sampling strategy for redundant objects. The study confirms there is no real standardisation in research designs regarding archaeological collections management however; it indicates that the phases of their projects are similarly structured to the English Heritage model (Figure 1).

Excavation

Archaeological project directors are required to record their decisions taken in the field with regard to their excavation strategy, field observations and provisional interpretations. In addition an assessment is made about the significance of artefacts, samples and contexts to provide answers to the research questions. As a result decisions are made about which artefacts, features and/or samples will be studied in more detail. This includes decisions about how to deal with exceptional artefacts (or finds), or finds not provided for in the research design and for which a budget may not have been planned. Because archaeological excavation is planned work that contributes to a project's objectives, one of the goals is to create data sets for artefact classes which answer specific research questions. To achieve this a work plan based on the project design is used in

---

[6] The survey involved 32 senior archaeologists who direct, or had directed projects in Afghanistan, Cyprus, Egypt, Greece, Iran, Israel, Jordan, Lebanon, Sicily, Syria and Turkey. This rating scale was used to analyse participant responses: 100–80 = Very high; 79–60 = High; 59–40 = Moderate; 39–20 = Low; 19–0 = Very low.

Phases of work	Documentation	Specifications	Resources
Phase 1: Project planning	PROJECT DESIGN	Project management techniques	Teams and team meetings
			Estimating
			Controlling time and money: the work plan
			Resource accounting
			Monitoring
			Project management packages
			Background
			Aims and objectives
			Methodology
			Resources and timetable
Phase 2: Fieldwork	SITE ARCHIVE	Site archive specification	Materials and records
			Matrix and summaries
	ASSESSMENT REPORT	Assessment report specification	Factual data
			Statement of potential (value of data listed)
			Storage and curation
Phase 3: Assessment of potential for analysis	UPDATED PROJECT DESIGN	Updated project design specification	Summary statement of potential
			Aims and objectives
			Publication and presentation
			Methods statement
			Resources and programming
Phase 4: Analysis and report preparation	RESEARCH ARCHIVE	Research archive specification	Catalogues and other records
	REPORT TEXT FOR PUBLICATION		Analytical reports
Phase 5: Dissemination	PROJECT ARCHIVE FOR DEPOSITION	Guidelines for the preparation of published reports	Minimum requirements
			Report-writing criteria
	PUBLICATION	Guidelines for the preparation of published reports	Production criteria

Figure 1: Phases of English Heritage (MoRPHE) model.

international models. Work includes recording different parameters in the field, such as collecting, registering and processing artefacts and samples and finishing the fieldwork.[7] Ideally, artefacts and samples are processed and sorted within conditions that optimally safeguard their condition and stability. The outcome is the creation of primary data and observations.

To achieve accuracy a very high percentage of archaeologists brief their core team, site staff and relevant consultants on data collection policies (Appendix 2). Likewise, recovery policies and on-site procedures are explained to excavators. In addition, collective and individual training is undertaken to ensure policies are understood and systems are in place for detecting cataloguing errors made during fieldwork.

Post-Excavation

Artefact retention or discard policies are determined by the research objectives of a project. Protocols often vary according to the specific needs and requirements of a particular project. Normally, policies reflect how and why individual artefacts and types of artefacts are retained, discarded or sampled during an investigation. A distinction is made between general, complex and vulnerable artefacts. Identifying artefact categories makes specialist research possible in the post-excavation phase. A unique number that consists of a distinctive combination of data, i.e. trench number, level or locus, and a serial number, will be allocated by an excavator to 'special finds' or 'small finds' in the field. Typically after an initial visual assessment is made by the project director at the end of each day, artefacts displaying diagnostic characteristics will later be registered in an artefact register or inventory.[8]

Documentation reflecting this information is shown daily to governmental representatives who at the end of the excavation season select items from the list of artefacts for accession by museums. This initial assessment helps to inform decisions about possible preservation treatments by on-site conservators. A copy of the 'custody list' is given by the project director to the governmental representative at the end of each season. General bulk items, such as pottery sherds, are not listed and may be stored or discarded. Survey responses indicate that space occupied by excavated material is on average $175m^2$. In some cases, at the end of each season archaeologists have little or no control over any artefacts once they have been accessioned into government-run storage depots or museums. A very high percentage of projects have on-site storage depots or facilities nearby, and 59% of archaeologists indicated their storage arrangements are adequate for

---

[7] Lee 2006, 55; see also Willems and Brandt 2004, 133.
[8] This may involve other staff, i.e. registrars, conservators, artefact specialists, photographers, and the project director.

short and long-term use. 23% indicate that storage was for short-term use only, whereas 18% were unsure of how long they would have access to storage.[9]

Almost half of archaeologists have 1–25% of inventoried artefacts accessioned by local museums, whereas the remaining half had 76–100% accessioned. More than half of the museums that archaeologists deal with have formal guidelines regarding accessioning artefacts and collections, and more than half of the archaeologists supplied museums with written notification of on-site conservation treatments that were provided prior to accessioning.

Preservation and Re-Use

Conserving artefacts is an integral part of the archaeological process, and requires specialist training, although not all archaeological projects employ qualified conservators; lack of funding may be a contributing factor. Often conservators assist project directors in establishing the needs and priorities of the project by providing input for policies and procedures for safe recovery, recording and artefact processing. Passive and active preservation are the two forms of treatment employed on-site. Passive preservation conditions the environment of an artefact so that deterioration is minimal during short- and long-term storage. Active preservation treats the artefact itself in such a way that further deterioration under storage conditions is minimal. The aim is to stabilise the artefact with all the information it holds. If impossible, the information present in the artefact is recorded while unprocessed material is sampled for later analysis. Time constraints, or other factors, may contribute to unprocessed material being stored. Before artefacts are treated, the initial situation is recorded by conservators as thoroughly as possible. Technical aspects are also documented as well as possible during the preservation process. In the case of preservation, the aim is maximum reversibility.[10]

Conservators select objects for conservation based on the aims and objectives of the project, as determined by the project director and specialists. Consideration is given to an artefact's state of preservation, storage space, time and funding. The survey of conservators found that on average 154 artefacts are conserved each season per site (Appendix 2). A high percentage of conservators are in favour of keeping all artefacts or parts of archaeological collections in their entirety in perpetuity. In some Middle Eastern countries the only catalogue or inventory of accessioned artefacts held by museums is found in handwritten paper journals, while in others this information is also retained in computer files. Project directors are not required to provide full details of non-registered artefacts that constitute

---
[9] Short-term = less than 5 years; long-term = 5–20 years.
[10] Pedeli and Pulga 2013; see also Stanley Price 1995; Sease 1994; 1992.

the majority of excavated material, therefore this lack of information inhibits knowledge of the values of the site for local governments. Furthermore, in many countries details of conservation assessments and treatments is not required. Guidelines based on conservation principles for transitioning (i.e. packing, transporting and depositing) artefacts from archaeological sites to museums have not been extensively developed in the Middle East. In many cases, actual conservation treatments performed by on-site project conservators may be the only treatments that excavated artefacts ever receive. Figure 2 lists the factors governing conservation priorities.

A very high percentage of conservators are trained in archaeological excavation techniques, and they comment that museums accessioned half of the conserved artefacts from their sites. Furthermore, 78% of conservators give advice to governments about the conservation interventions they perform, while 89% provide advice for long-term care of artefacts and collections. Figure 3 shows how conservators prepare archaeological artefacts for long-term storage.

The objective of depositing archaeological artefacts and collections into museums and repositories is to achieve sustainable preservation of the information pertaining to archaeological sites *ex situ* for the benefit of future research and people's perception of the archaeological heritage.[11] This is achieved by preserving, managing and safeguarding archaeological objects and original documentation so that the condition of the material remains as stable as possible. This process involves local governmental requirements and those of the museum itself. Policies for these procedures and processes are underdeveloped in many countries. For instance, while 80% of curators indicated that their museums/repositories request a catalogue of objects and copies of field records, photographs and maps, only 27% of museums request objects in a stabilised and/or conserved condition, and 20% of museums have guidelines for packing artefacts. 20% enter into curation agreements with archaeologists, while just 10% specify their expectations for delivery of artefacts, but 92% of museums held academic archaeological collections. 57% of museums have contact with archaeologists prior to excavations but only half receive advice detailing expected volumes of artefacts. 15% of curators receive advice detailing conservation treatments and 40% of museums are involved in the excavation process

---

[11] Willems and Brandt 2004, 179.

Participant code no.	Conservator Q.1.2. What factors govern your priorities when conserving artefacts?
CO001	My priority is bronze objects, then Neolithic pottery, also rarity of objects and to consolidate the fragile objects.
CO003	Ensure long term stability and proper storage.
CO004	From the conservator's point of view, the factors were related to the condition of the objects and whether there was the need to be conserved, or packed properly before being drawn, photographed or stored.
CO005	Condition. Experts present for length of stay. Scheduling, rarity, potential of deterioration.
CO006	For artefacts, it's a discussion between the relevant research teams i.e. with faunal there has been an emphasis on horn cores/craniums. These have been a priority.
CO007	Generally the priorities were governed by the material needs (i.e. organic artefacts that required immediate stabilisation), rarity of artefacts (e.g. coinage that was desired for immediate examination), and usefulness in archaeological dating.
CO008	On excavations priorities were assigned in consultation with archaeologists. They depend on a combination of importance of objects/context/condition. Considerations include time, equipment and materials limitations. In prioritising treatment, the need for the objects to be treated and moved on to illustrators and photographers in limited time is taken into account.
CO009	Condition, context, respect for integrity of object, reversibility, safety, facilitates, competence, funding, and suitability of treatment.
CO010	It depends on the artefact and the contract. Usually, the principal factor to be taken into account is the preservation state of the artefact and its final destination. Additionally, when it comes to the use of toxic substances (i.e. BTA as a stabilisation treatment), the priority is the safety of the user and the proper storage of chemicals.
CO011	I take into consideration: 1. all ethical structures pertaining to professional conservation; 2. the potential research uses for the artefact, which may or may not include instrumental analysis; 3. the likelihood of instrumental analysis and sampling, and whether that will happen on a macro or micro scale (always aware that analytical methods improve with time and unforeseeable analytical methods will become available and common); 4. the likely storage conditions for the artifact in the future; 5. whether or not the artefact is likely to be a museum display object.
CO012	First of all to examine the material of an artefact, whether is vulnerable or unstable or not and to divide the artefacts according to their material and their needs. Then to keep documents by taking photos and complete a conditional report form. The next is to ensure a suitable and safe environment to save the objects. The target is to avoid the shock and to preserve the artefacts till the time of their systematic conservation. If there is a need, first aid conservation interventions should be taking place in this stage. During systematic treatment, reversibility and minimal intervention are the principles that govern my actions.

FIGURE 2: CONSERVATION CONSIDERATIONS.

Participant code no.	Conservator Q.2.6. How do you prepare archaeological artefacts for long-term storage?
CO001	Avoid the conditions of corrosion and provide a suitable environment (humidity, heating, pure air not polluted).
CO003	Use readily available packing material generally. For small objects (metal, glass): polythene air tight boxes, bubble wrap, acid free paper. For larger objects: cardboard boxes, polystyrene chips and boards, bubble wrap.
CO004	It depends on the material and the storage available. My focus is on using inert materials to isolate the objects from their environment in order to create a stable environment for their long-term preservation. Packing and storage materials are always a priority when organising a season. If there is need the objects are lightly cleaned and in case of metals which present signs of active corrosion, the objects might be stabilised chemically (if there is need and such process is possible) or packed with silica gel. In most cases the objects are just lightly cleaned and packed properly.
CO005	Metals - stored in polystyrene containers purchased in Australia with silica gel conditioned to 10% RH and sealed with (zip lock bags perforated for air exchange) humidity card visible on the side. Ceramics - large into wooden crates, padding provided by old bags in new (accession # on object). For all small finds - in zip lock bags - datable numbered on bag and on separate card and in small non-archival cardboard locking boxes/shoe boxes.
CO006	Depends on size, material etc. Is a case by case relationship. I liaise with the Finds Officer and work with her expectations.
CO007	Metal artefacts were stored in polypropylene containers with dry silica gel. Small finds were stored with either polyethylene foam or acid-free tissue in polypropylene containers. Larger finds and ceramics were padded and stored in wooden trays. Bulk sherds were marked and bagged.
CO008	If not handed over to a museum then packing in acid-free tissue for small/fragile objects in suitable containers or plastic bags. Pottery in crates, trays on metal shelving. Purpose-made supports are used when required (providing polyeth. foam etc available). Metals packed in silica gel have to be particularly carefully sealed - almost impossible.
CO010	It depends on the material, the size of the artefact, the preservation state, the storage area if it keeps the proper environmental conditions. I pay more attention to create the proper environment than intervene to the object itself.
CO011	In general, I try to stabilise the artefact both physically and chemically, provide good support, and buffer against storage conditions that I know will be uncontrolled.
CO012	It depends on the material of an artefact. Organic and inorganic materials should be kept in different environmental conditions. And again there should be more diversity of the conditions depending on the material. For example metals should be kept in an environment with very low humidity, but ceramics on the other hand could be storage in higher concentrations. Organics need no light, low temperature and middle range humidity.

FIGURE 3: PREPARATION FOR LONG-TERM STORAGE.

Archaeological Collections Management Practice

What is Archaeological Collections Management Practice?

Archaeological collections management practice incorporates all specific tasks that are undertaken for the care and preservation of artefacts. The aim of a collections management system should be to develop a sustainable material archive for current and future research for each archaeological site. Archaeological material should be stored and packed so it is protected from the environment, to prevent damage and limit degradation.[12] At archaeological sites during an excavation season good archaeological management practice involves allocating resources and performing actions to care for and preserve physical objects and the accompanying data. It also involves attending to the physical issues of conservation, access and use and inventory.[13] These tasks in many cases are performed by a site registrar, conservator or other nominated staff members or combinations of these. It is a role that may take a number of seasons to learn fully depending on the complexity of the system(s) employed at a site.

Planning for the Creation of Collections

The study found that archaeological project directors are divided in their opinions about keeping all parts of collections in perpetuity.[14] This suggests that adequate planning is required, whether keeping or discarding material. At a fundamental level when an artefact is recovered it is assessed on whether it is relevant, however decisions to keep or not will depend on the range of options and potential issues involved. The condition of an artefact is considered in regard to allocating resources that allow early analysis and design activities to commence in a focussed manner, with conclusions and recommendations for the post-excavation storage phase. Figure 4 outlines the areas and shows how a 'built in' collections management system can be organised within an overall site management plan.[15]

Governance

Archaeological project directors conducting archaeological activities are governed by the rules, regulations and legislative requirements of a country in which the archaeological activity takes place and those of their universities and/or funding institutions. Activities conducted at World Heritage Sites (listed and tentative)

---

[12] Cassidy and Guerre 2009. Çatalhöyük Finds Guidance.
[13] U.S. National Park Service 2016. Glossary. https://www.nps.gov/archeology/collections/glossary.htm (14/07/2016).
[14] Fitzpatrick 2015.
[15] Adapted from Sullivan 1995, 15-26.

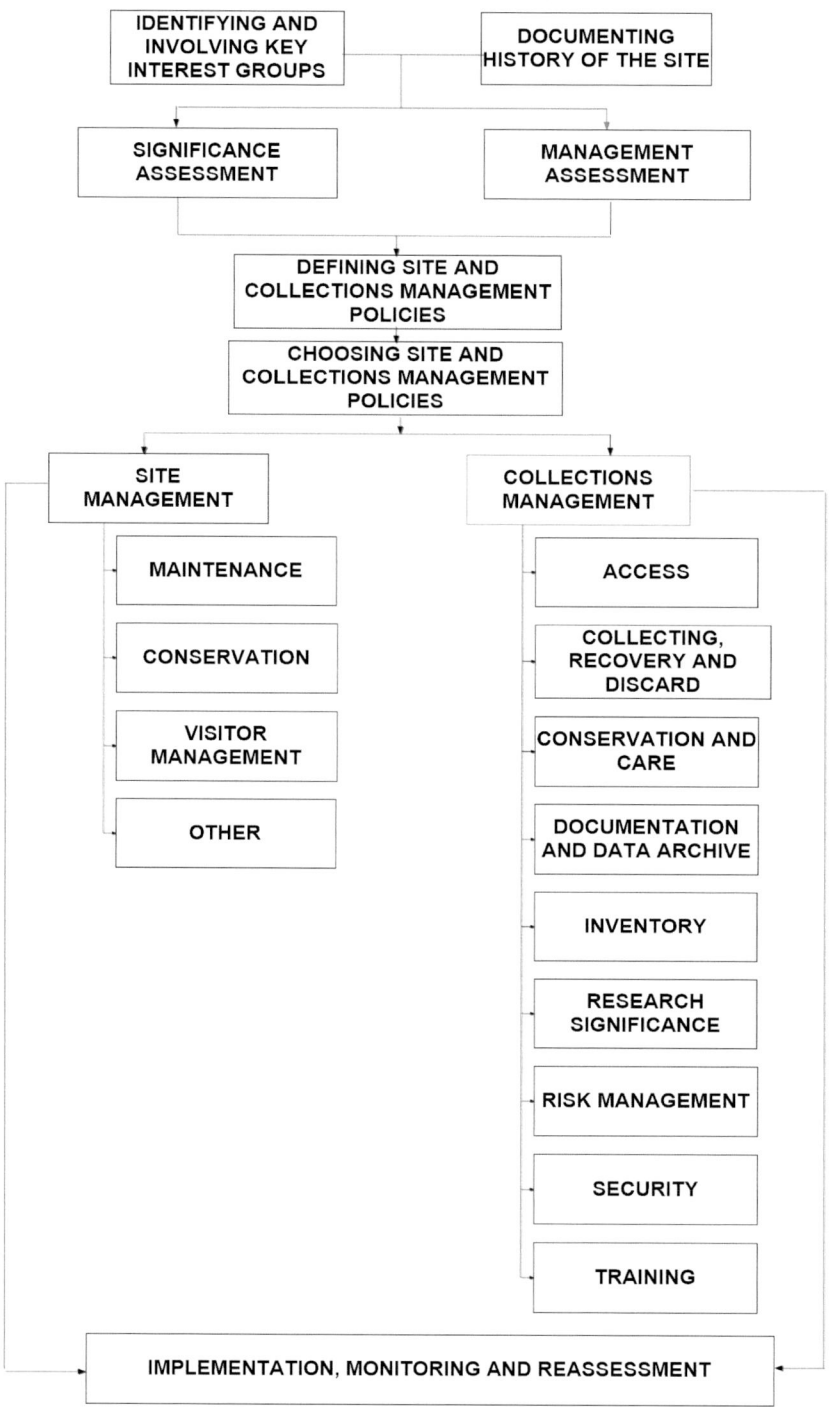

FIGURE 4: ARCHAEOLOGICAL COLLECTIONS MANAGEMENT SYSTEM.

are further subject to guidelines and charters in order to retain their values when countries are signatories. Increasingly, Middle Eastern governments aim to conserve and preserve heritage values while developing sustainable cultural tourism-related industries. In addition to reducing permit fees by up to 50% for projects that undertake preservation work, this conservation-led change is reflected in Jordan's new regulations by redefining archaeological activities that focus on conservation, rehabilitation, recording and training:[16]

- Excavations: Scientific excavations at the archaeological site.
- Surveys: Scientific documentation of the archaeological remains that are visible on the surface.
- Salvage/rescue projects: Surveys and excavations works in endangered and exposed archaeological areas where construction or other development works or natural factors have uncovered archaeological material.
- Scientific research projects: Systematic scientific research projects with excavation and survey activities and with defined, executable aims and detailed, scheduled plans.
- Conservation and restoration projects: Scientific projects proposed for the restoration, conservation and reconstruction at an archaeological site, using scientific methods and techniques within a defined and specific plan.
- Excavation training projects: Projects undertaken by Jordanian and foreign universities and institutes which offer academic programs in the field of archaeology, i.e. for the purposes of training students in the techniques of excavation in conjunction with the Department.
- Archaeological documentation projects: Projects which document archaeological sites using modern techniques.
- Rehabilitation and management of archaeological sites projects: Projects which rehabilitate, develop and manage archaeological sites.[17]

Collections Management Strategies

But although Jordan's new regulations suggest that the Ministry of Tourism aims to implement sustainable conservation and preservation measures for archaeological sites, the mechanisms to include managing archaeological collections for doing so are absent. This is seen in Article 5(c), where there are no specific guidelines or references to a 'standard' for documenting artefacts, and the structural requirements for site plans are not clear. References to managing archaeological collections are somewhat vague, i.e. applicants for permits for archaeological projects must have 'sufficient experience in storing and safeguarding antiquities discovered in the course of excavation, such as registration, documentation and classification.' Consequently, project directors conducting archaeological activities in Jordan and

---

[16] Hashemite Kingdom of Jordan 2012. Regulations for Archaeological Projects in Jordan pursuant to Law No. 21 as amended 1988.
[17] Jordanian Directorate of Antiquities 2015.

in many other Middle Eastern countries are not legally required to develop written policies and procedures for excavation, field artefact recovery, or field laboratory protocols. The same can be said for developing written guidelines for recording in field notebooks and recording forms. Without documented details on how procedural aspects related to the archaeological process should be conducted, this lack of systemisation can affect how archaeological artefacts and collections are managed in the long-term, i.e. because of misunderstandings and misinterpretations. The main process phases on which policy development should focus are:

- Locational, excavation and recording methodologies
- Collecting, conserving, storage, occupational health and safety
- Processing, washing, drying, registering, classifying, analysing
- Primary data creation and storage

Phases of Archaeological Process

At case study sites the archaeological collections consisted of two components – the documentation and records, and the physical objects themselves (Appendix 1). The site policies for the archaeological processes determined what the procedures should be in relation to the two above components. At all case study sites, the aim of recovering the artefacts was to quantify, order and index what was recovered in a consistent manner. A diagrammatic flowchart which set out the entire archaeological process was employed at site No. 4.[18] This 'triage' system is documented through a visual interpretation which sets out the overall policies for how artefacts are processed from the point of recovery to their eventual discard. It further sets out the stages in between whereby artefact types are sorted according to quality and condition, then recorded and stored. These policies are supported by detailed written procedures in a Season Field Manual.[19] The collections management process describes how artefacts are categorised, the stages of assessment, recording, conservation, review, discard and storage. It further highlights how data are collected and entered into specific artefact-type databases (i.e. pottery, bone) which are in turn linked to the central project database and site archive.[20]

All sites, including those with a 'no discard' policy, discard at least some archaeological material. Informal assessments of the potential for analyses are conducted prior to allocation to a field laboratory. During the recovery phase, the significance or further potential of an object is determined by a second, closer review of the characteristics of the artefact combined with consideration of the written contextual data. Depending on the nature of a site and the way in which each project is organised, this review is performed by either a project director, a

---

[18] Tell Ta'yinat, Turkey.
[19] Ta'yinat Season Field Manual 2006.
[20] Ta'yinat Archaeological Project website 2016. http://sites.utoronto.ca/tap/ (05/08/2016).

conservator, registrar or other specialist(s). Once the potential of any artefact is established the documents and artefacts are then stored to await specialist analyses. At sites where archaeological specialists are present this process can begin immediately, otherwise artefacts are stored until specialists are available. The post-excavation phase requires strategies for adequate short-term storage, care and security of artefacts, in addition to procedures for access by researchers. Written procedures for field laboratory processes are distributed to on-site personnel at sites Nos. 3 and 4.[21]

Written or Formal Policies

The 2006 Season Field Manual employed at Tell Ta'yinat outlines policies and procedures for excavation techniques, field artefact recovery actions, and field laboratory methods, in addition to guidelines for completing documentation. Another site has a number of documented policies and procedures for excavators to follow, and for how collected artefacts are handled, packed and stored; a further site circulated instruction sheets to students with details of the daily work routine. A further site held student training sessions on pottery typologies prior to excavation (Appendix 1).

Conserving and Caring for Archaeological Collections

A summary of the preventive conservation treatments conducted on accessioned objects was forwarded to the relevant antiquities authorities with the artefacts by three case study sites.[22] However, advice was not given about future artefact care to museum staff, but this is not a legal requirement. It was not determined whether the overall conditions of on-site collections were reported on annually. It was also not known whether parts of collections in poor condition, or parts which were at most risk, were reported on. Case study sites in Turkey were legally obliged to conduct annual inventories of artefacts held in the on-site storage areas. This was not the case in Syria, thus, year-to-year comparisons were not possible and accurate knowledge of what was stored on-site was not apparent.

Specialised Environmental Storage

Interventive conservation treatment on pottery and metal artefacts was observed at four case study sites.[23] This process involved cleaning, removing accretions, and in some cases applying a coating of wax to artefacts that were identified in the field as 'special finds'. This decision-making process involved the project director and/or the conservator, usually on a daily basis, after new artefacts were registered. The

---

[21] Çatalhöyük Research Project and Ta'yinat Archaeological Project, Turkey.
[22] Jebel Khalid, Syria; Çatalhöyük, Turkey; and Tell Ta'yinat, Turkey.
[23] Jebel Khalid, Syria; Catalhoyuk, Turkey; Tell Ta'yinat, Turkey; and Antiochia ad Cragum, Turkey.

aim of interventive treatment is to stabilise an artefact without removing evidence of its history. Figure 5 summarizes the basic recommended methods of treatment and storage for archaeological artefacts as recommended by the Museum of London Archaeology Service.[24] Artefacts listed in the 'Material' column were observed at the case study sites. In the 'Storage' column, dry storage is recommended for all artefacts with the exception of glass, horn, ivory, resin and wood. Dry storage was observed at all case study sites. Clay and clay related artefacts comprise approximately 25% of surveyed collections, whereas human and faunal bone comprises some 38%. These two figures combined constitute more than 60% of the entire stored collections. This means that the remaining 40% of a site's storage space holds a range of artefacts more diverse. It suggests that some artefacts may require specialised storage, such as long-term wet-storage areas. Wet-storage areas were not observed on-site. Specialised storage facilities equivalent to 'museum standards' which take into account the effects of physical forces, fire, water, criminal activities, pests, contaminants, light and UV radiation, incorrect temperature, incorrect relative humidity or dissociation were not observed at the sites.[25]

Material	Treatment	Storage
Antler	Wash	Dry
Bone	Wash	Dry
Copper	Do not clean	Dry
Ceramic[1]	Wash	Dry
Fibre	Do not clean	Dry
Flint artefacts[2]	Gentle wash	Dry
Glass (if stable)	Wash	Dry (wet if unstable)
Gold	Wash	Dry
Horn	Gentle wash	Wet
Iron	Do not clean	Dry (desiccated)
Ivory	Do not clean	Wet
Lead	Do not wash	Dry (desiccated)
Leather	Gentle wash	Wet
Plaster (painted wall)	Damp sponge	Dry
Resin (amber)	Do not clean	Wet
Shell	Gentle wash	Dry
Silver	Do not clean	Dry
Stone	Dry brush or wash	Dry
Wood	Gentle wash	Wet

[1] Pottery with lettering should not be washed nor should crucibles since they may contain residues.
[2] Burnt flint should be dry-brushed and stored dry.

FIGURE 5: RECOMMENDATIONS FOR POST-EXAMINATION ARTEFACT TREATMENT AND STORAGE.

[24] Grey 2006, 18-19. Adapted from Archaeological Finds Procedures Manual; see also Unruh 2001 and 2012.
[25] Waller 2014, 9. These criteria are used when considering the frequency and severity of catastrophic, severe or on-going risks to collections, or parts of collections, for the next 100 years; see also Waller 1994.

Archaeological Collections Management

Governance and Principles

Archaeological activities are regulated by the legislation of countries in which surveys or excavations are conducted. Non-compliance could lead to prosecution or permit suspension or refusal. The study found that archaeological project directors who conduct archaeological research in Turkey are subject to greater responsibilities and requirements than those who conduct archaeological research in Syria. Turkey's cultural heritage legislation contains more prescriptive instruments designed to preserve archaeological collections than other reviewed laws from North Africa, Southwest Asia and the Eastern Mediterranean. However, although Turkey's cultural heritage laws contain greater responsibilities for project directors than in neighbouring countries, they do not meet minimum international standards for archaeological collections management.

A plethora of international standards exists for the care and preservation of museum archaeological collections.[26] Figure 6 provides an example of international minimum standards for documenting archaeological collections.

---

[26] Lee 2006. *Management of Research Projects in the Historic Environment: The MoRPHE Project Managers Guide.* http//www.english-heritage.org.uk_publications_morphe-project-planning-note-6_morpheprojectplanningnote6.pdf (30/08/11); see also Poole *et al.* 2015, 6; Aslan 2014, 117; Australian Government 2014, *Australian Best Practice Guide to Collecting Cultural Material*; Golfomitsou and Rico 2014, 99; Heritage Council of Victoria 2014; Heritage Victoria 2014; Palumbo *et al.* 2014, 145; Commission of the European Communities 2013, 111; Doumas 2013, 109; ICOM 2013; Poole and Dawson 2013; Australian Association of Consulting Archaeologists 2012, *Code of Ethics;* English Heritage 2012; National Museum of Iceland 2012, 3-10*;* Standards Australia 2012, *Standards Australia Guide – Project Prioritisation Process and Criteria*; State Historical Society of North Dakota 2012; Watkins *et al.* 2012; Brown 2011, *Safeguarding Archaeological Information – Procedures for minimising risk to undeposited archaeological archives*; Directorate of Culture and Cultural and Natural Heritage, Strasbourg 2011, 70-71; Ertürk 2011, 336; Standards Australia International 2011, *Guide to Standards – Good Management Practice;* ICOMOS 2010; Ad hoc Group for Inventory and Documentation 2009; British Standards Institution 2009, *PAS 197:2009 Code of Practice for Cultural Collections Management*; California State Parks 2009*;* Museums and Galleries Commission 2009, *The Small Museums Cataloguing Manual*; Archaeological Institute of America 2008, *Code of Professional Standards*; Directorate of Culture and Cultural and Natural Heritage Regional Co-operation Division 2008, 213; English Heritage 2008, 38; Reibel 2008; Brown 2007, *Archaeological Archives. A guide to best practice in creation, compilation, transfer and curation;* ICOM 2004, *Running a Museum: A Practical Handbook;* UNESCO 2007; Van den Dries and Willems 2007; Willems and Van den Dries 2007, *Quality Management in Archaeology*; Baca *et al.* 2006; Bryn Mawr College 2006, *Collections Management Policy*; Grey 2006, *Archaeological Finds Procedures Manual*; Historic Scotland 2006, 1; National Park Service 2006, *Museum Handbook Part I Museum Collections*; Records Management Association of Australasia 2006; McIlwaine 2005; University of Melbourne 2005, *Policy on the Management of Research Data and Records*; Childs 2010; Tell Madaba Archaeological Project 2004, *Excavation Manual*; Willems and Brandt 2004, *Dutch Archaeology Quality Standard;* Getty Conservation Institute 2003; Standards Australia 2003, AS ISO 10013-2003 *Guidelines for quality management system documentation*; National Archives of Australia 2002; Perrin 2002; Standards Australia 2006, AS ISO 15489.1-2002 *Records Management Part 1: General*; Standards Australia 2002, AS ISO 15489.2- 2002 *Records Management Part 2*: Guidelines; Banning 2000, 129; ISO International 2000, *ISO Standard 9001*; National Park Service 2000, *Museum Handbook Part II Museum Records;* Greene 1999, 43; Griset and Kodack 1999, *Guidelines for the Field Collection of Archaeological Materials and Standard Operating Procedures for Curating Department of Defense Archaeological Collections*; United States Army Corps of Engineers 1999; Buck and Gilmore 1998; Heritage Collections Council 1998, *Managing Collections*;

Elements	Specifications
Research Design	The contribution the project is expected to make to archaeological knowledge in the context of the current framework of local, regional and national research. How significance criteria will be applied to artefacts and/or the site a) survival/condition, b) period, c) rarity, d) fragility/vulnerability, e) documentation; f) group value, g) potential. Any opportunities for integrating aspects of a project with related non-archaeological research (education and outreach programs). Likely possibilities for future research which may emerge from the project. Opportunities for experimental work.
Primary Data	Correspondence relating to fieldwork; survey reports (borehole, geophysical, documentary); site notebooks and/or diaries; original photographic records; site drawings (plans, sections, elevations); original context records; datasets relating to artefacts, ecofacts and any other sample residues; copies of original 'finds' records (registered finds, bulk finds, artefact dating catalogues; records of conservation and x-rays undertaken during fieldwork; original sample records; skeleton records; computer discs and printouts.
Observations	Full site matrix (all cross-checked stratigraphic relationships). Summary account of the artefact record (range, quality, condition and any other pertinent details of the artefact collection). Summary of the environmental record (range, quality, condition and any other pertinent details of the environmental material collected).
Data classes for each material category	Quantity of material and/or records likely to be produced for the project. Provenance of material, including comments on provisional dating and evidence for contamination of residuality. Range and variety of materials, including comments on any bias observed due to collection and sampling strategies. Condition of material, including comments on the extent to which an assemblage is likely to be affected by preservation bias and comment on its potential for long-term storage. Primary sources or relevant documentation which may enhance the study of site data.
Significance	Questions posed in the project design that the data-collection has the potential to answer. New research questions resulting from the data-collection. Potential value of the data-collection to local, regional and national research priorities.
Conservation long-term care and discard	Immediate and long-term conservation and storage requirements for the data held in the site archive. Discarding material from mixed, contaminated or unstratified contexts, where there is no apparent purpose in retention. How discard policy demonstrates due regard for the views of the eventual recipient of the archive, the legal owners of the material and those responsible for the care of the excavated site.

FIGURE 6 INTERNATIONAL MINIMUM STANDARDS FOR DOCUMENTING ARCHAEOLOGICAL COLLECTIONS.

National Park Service 1998, *Museum Handbook Part III Museum Collections Use;* Willems *et al.* 1997; Pearce 1996, 1992, 2990; CIDOC 1995, *International Guidelines for Museum Object Information;* Society of Museum Archaeologists 1995, 1993; Stanley-Price 1995; Sease 1999, 1994; Society of Museum Archaeologists 1993; Museums and Galleries Commission 1992; Pearce 1992, *Managing Archaeological Resources from the Museum Perspective*; Sullivan 1992; American Association of Museums 2004, 2003, 1984, *Caring for Collections: Strategies for Conservation, Maintenance and Documentation*; Singley 1981.

However, the effective application of such standards at archaeological sites depends on whether project directors are familiar with them, whether they are indeed practical, and the allocation of resources needed to maintain such systems. At one of the case study sites it took a team of three collections management personnel, including a registrar and a conservator, to manage the system and the logistical realities which occur as a result of the handling, cataloguing, registration and documentation processes. Despite a high level of commitment and the existence of specific protocols for processing and accessing artefacts and collections, problems can exist in terms of being able to keep track of and locate artefacts. Losing track of artefacts occurs when objects are either in the process of being analysed, or conserved in specialist laboratories, were misplaced or dissociated, or had gone missing.

Ultimately, the archaeological project directors are responsible for the security and standard of care that the artefacts and collections receive. Likewise, directors are responsible for further decisions to retain or discard archaeological material, although reference to discard is not made in any reviewed legislation or regulations. Some projects discard non-diagnostic sherds while others do not. It was observed that after certain characteristics (i.e. fabric types, weights, etc.) of non-diagnostics are documented the items are then discarded. These objects are perceived as having no further research value. The recorded information is considered adequate for any future analytical purposes although samples are retained of those discarded. Artefacts to be stored have analytical and further value for their contributions to type-series or study collections. Those kept for analyses include diagnostic pieces, whole objects or small finds. Decisions about what to keep and what to discard vary at archaeological sites and these decisions in some way are influenced by logistical considerations, i.e. available storage space.

The standard of care and preservation that excavated artefacts receive before going into long-term storage depots will depend on informal and formal collections management policies. It will also depend on the allocation of resources within the greater archaeological project. At some sites this is very much a conservation-led process. In-field collecting and post-excavation procedures reflect varied levels of planning and resourcing, and the short and long-term application of dedicated resources for managing artefacts is varied. Some project directors regard the allocation of resources for post-excavation care and preservation as just as important as the other phases of the process, whereas others do not. This is demonstrated by the condition and status of stored collections. Many tonnes of archaeological material have been excavated and are being stored under a range of varying conditions. Although similar in structure to international models for managing a 'project', whereby there are distinct stages of excavation, processing, initial recording, assessment and analysis, archiving and storing, there is no standardisation of collections management methodologies.

Current Management, Strategies and Approaches

An organisational hierarchy existed at all case study sites and all personnel are accountable to the project directors, who determine policies regarding how artefacts are recovered, processed and stored. At two of the sites policies were developed in close consultation with the site conservator(s). The policies reflect a conservation-led process, beginning with documented procedures from recovery to post-excavation treatment. At the majority of sites conservators are involved in an initial assessment of recovered objects based on the stability and condition of the artefact. Policies and procedures about artefact recovery techniques and post-excavation processes are either made clear to excavators, specialists and workers, either verbally or through written instructions. This is communicated either personally by the project director or through the chain of command via core supervising personnel. Project directors are all senior academics affiliated with universities and/or archaeological institutes, and all have had previous experience in directing other archaeological projects. They are assisted by varying numbers of core personnel or staff who maintain the overall view of the project's objectives.

It is undetermined whether formal organisational charts exist for staff, outlining their roles and credentials, and assessing the amount of time spent on forward planning by staff was beyond the scope of the study, as was reviewing organisational techniques by which project directors monitored their projects. Likewise the frequency of staff meetings to monitor progress and ensure expenditure is in line with forecasts is undetermined, as was obtaining data about planned and on-going adjustments to priorities, methodologies, timetabling and budgets. Information on whether staff meet regularly to ensure work is being carried out to an appropriate professional standard was not obtained, or if records are made of progress reports at staff meetings. It was undetermined whether information of this nature is circulated to all concerned, or if project directors implement formal means for identifying and evaluating risks to their collections.

All project directors were granted permits to excavate for the respective season in which the study was conducted, however the granting of permits is not guaranteed and they must be re-applied for each year. The project director of each case study site expressed concern about the permit application process and the likelihood of refusal. Two examples of this were observed in Syria in 2010 and in Turkey in 2013, both of which did not receive their permits until after international teams of approximately 60 personnel had arrived in the countries.[27]

Project directors have authority over, and are ultimately responsible for staff, students and volunteers working at their projects. However all project directors reported

---

[27] Jebel Khalid, Syria and Antiochia ad Cragum, Turkey.

regularly to governmental representatives who oversee and monitor on-site activities daily. Each case study site had one to three assistant directors affiliated with other universities. Each project director and assistant director specialises in various areas of research and most participated in the field season. Their specialties predominantly include ceramics, pottery typologies, classical architecture and archaeometric testing and studies. Additional archaeological specialists attend sites, some of whom had been conducting research at that particular site for many years. It was beyond the scope of the study to determine when and how representatives of each specialist area within the projects are consulted, or when the project director conducts forward planning. It was also unknown whether reference is made to records of time and cost performance from previous years. The participation of archaeological specialists is dependent upon the nature of a site, the characteristics of the artefacts being recovered and the research focus of the project. All but case study site No. 1 contain multiple occupation periods spanning various historic periods.[28]

Specialist attendance on-site during an excavation or study season was dependent upon the project's work plan, the budget and the specialist's availability. Permanent and/or temporary laboratories were observed at all case study sites. The laboratories include dedicated work places and equipment, such as computers and scientific instruments. These include spaces for object registration and storage and conservation. At one site use was made of permanent collections management personnel, whereas at other sites artefacts were registered by the project director or a temporary registrar. Four sites employed on-site conservators for part or all of the excavation seasons, and some 200 personnel were attached to the largest site in 2012.[29] By comparison, some 12 personnel were attached to the smallest case study site in 2010.[30] A site management plan nominating a start and finish date of the project existed at one site and this site employed a schedule outlining the tasks to be performed for the excavation season and for the order in which they would be performed.

Artefacts in Archaeologial Collections

Pottery, lithics, bone (human and faunal), soil and registered objects are the broad artefact categories which are recovered at each site. Metals and glass are generally included as registered artefacts. Artefacts are predominantly stored in standard-sized plastic crates or non-standard wooden or cardboard boxes according to material types, by year of excavation and locus. These categories are further sub-divided into typologies for the purpose of analyses. Artefact classifications depend on the site type, on the research focus at each site and on the attendance of specialists. Categorisation includes types and sub-types of pottery and other

---

[28] Jebel Khalid is an Hellenistic site with no other occupation phases.
[29] Çatalhöyük, Turkey.
[30] Tell Ahmar, Syria.

clay artefacts, metal, glass and faience, plaster and stone or sculptural fragments, faunal remains, palaeobotanical remains, wood and other organics, soil and radiocarbon samples. Delicate, unstable and/or more uncommon objects are stored in locked laboratories, with the exception of those accessioned into local regional museums. At all case study sites the greatest numbers of artefacts were pottery (clay-based) objects and bone elements.

Documentation System and Digital Archive

It was observed that the size and volume of the site archive is influenced by the objectives of the project, its scope and the budget. All case study sites produce a full site matrix by which stratigraphic relationships can be cross-checked and the stratigraphic sequences of the site established. The Harris Matrix method is most commonly used. It was not determined whether the site archive includes a statement describing the range, quality and condition or any other pertinent details of the 'non-registered' artefact collections.

All case study sites create files and records which consist of data specifying the name and location, including a grid reference of the site.[31] Records include the year in which the project began and maps. Specifics of the periods and site types are recorded together with details of whether excavations are conducted continuously since the commencement of the projects. Details specifying previous work conducted at the sites is included, however, a specific location of site archives was undetermined. A review of any formal agreements for access to the sites was beyond the scope of the study, as was obtaining knowledge concerning any arrangements for compensation or reinstatement to landowners.

Storage Provision and Future Expansion Needs

There is no legal requirement for on-site storage depots to be constructed at archaeological sites in Syria; however, it is compulsory for archaeological project directors working in Turkey to do so. In both countries there are no legislated building specifications or storage configuration guidelines.[32] Legislation does not contain specifications for assessments which determine the immediate and long-term conservation and storage requirements for (a) data held in the site archive, or for (b) suitable facilities for excavated artefacts. Physical artefacts and collections are predominantly stored in standard-sized plastic crates and/or non-standard-sized plastic, wooden or cardboard boxes. Assorted sizes of archive-quality plastic containers are used. Large artefacts are typically stored individually on shelves or directly on the floor at each site. The study found

---

[31] Richards and Robinson 2000; see also Bryson 2016.
[32] Republic of Turkey, 2012. *Rules & Principles for Conducting Survey, Sondage and Excavations on Cultural and Natural Heritage*. Article 7(1) f.

that no project directors had knowledge of how many kilograms of artefacts or numbers of crates of artefacts are accumulated annually at their site. This means that predicting future expansion needs accurately is somewhat difficult for them. With the exception of two, the other case study sites made use of empty private, ex-government or farm buildings or rooms already located on or near their sites.[33] Likewise, the numbers of containers that hold artefacts that are stored in on-site facilities and the actual space that the containers occupied was unknown. There is no legal requirement in Syria or many other countries to conduct an annual artefact and collection(s) inventory. Absent from legislation are specifications for storage buildings which take into account the duration of a project or the space which will be required over a given period of time. Also absent are descriptive measures for controlling the internal environment of storage depots or for security systems and controls. Formal agreements for where and how excavated material and records will be deposited and curated are not entered into between the Syrian or Turkish governments and archaeological project directors.

Levels of Use of the Collections

The study suggested that maintaining associations with, and connections to all components of collections that are accessioned into local museums is problematic both for archaeological project directors and for museum staff. Typically, a 'custody list' of artefacts with photographs and summaries written by trench supervisors of the season's findings accompanied artefacts. Relocating artefacts for research purposes, particularly in Syria, is difficult as the custody list is transferred by hand into single-copy paper ledgers. This is also the case in Turkey; however, regional museums, such as the Konya Archaeological Museum, have a computing system into which this data is duplicated. The handwritten documentation system made locating artefacts difficult. Researchers wishing to access artefacts in on-site storage depots may only gain entry during the excavation season. Applications for access to objects in museums must be made through local directorates well in advance due to the length of time it takes to process requests and to locate objects. Figure 7 provides an example of the research categories and numbers of participating specialists at a Neolithic site from 2003 to 2012. In Syria and Turkey, it is not compulsory for project directors to furnish copies of a full site archive or documents such as data sets, field diaries, archaeometric test results, specialist reports or the like. This makes it difficult for museum staff to provide comprehensive information for exhibited artefacts given the limited information that archaeological project directors are legally obliged to provide. Neither Syrian nor Turkish directorates enter into formal agreements for access to artefacts and/or collections with project directors.

---

[33] Tell Ahmar, Syria and Çatalhöyük, Turkey.

Research category	Çatalhöyük Specialist Personnel									
	2003	2004	2005	2006	2007	2008	2009	2010	2011	2012
Architectural analysis	-	1	4	2	1	1	1	1	-	-
C14 dating and isotopic analysis	-	-	1	1	-	3	2	3	-	-
Ceramics and pottery	2	1	4	4	6	3	2	3	4	9
Charcoal	-	1	-	-	-	1	-	1	1	1
Chipped stone and lithics	3	6	2	4	2	4	3	5	4	11
Clay architectural analysis and hearths	-	-	-	-	-	1	1	1	-	2
Clay balls and geometric shapes, clay beads	-	2	-	-	-	2	2	2	1	1
Clay materiality and sourcing	-	-	-	1	1	1	2	1	1	1
Clay stamps	-	1	1	-	-	-	1	-	-	-
Ethnoarchaeology, textiles, basketry and social anthropology	7	3	1	-	-	-	1	-	-	-
Fauna	6	7	11	12	10	7	7	2	4	13
Figurines and miniature clay objects	-	2	2	2	2	2	3	3	4	4
Forensics and Chemical analysis	-	-	-	-	-	5	4	2	-	-
Ground stone and bead technology	-	1	2	2	5	1	2	5	2	3
Heavy residue	2	1	1	2	2	1	2	2	2	1
Human remains	3	8	7	10	12	5	12	7	3	13
Landscape survey and coring	-	-	-	-	-	4	3	-	-	-
Microfauna and micromorphology	-	3	1	3	-	-	3	4	1	4
Palaeoethnobotany, phytoliths and starch residue	4	5	8	9	13	11	9	7	7	25
Post-chalcolithic assemblage	-	-	-	-	-	-	-	-	2	2
Shell	-	-	-	-	-	2	3	2	-	-
Speleothem sourcing and sub-surface imaging	-	-	-	-	-	3	2	-	2	2
Systems	-	-	-	-	-	-	-	-	-	4
Visualisation	-	-	-	-	-	-	5	6	8	8

FIGURE 7: RESEARCH CATEGORIES AND PARTICIPATING SPECIALISTS 2003-2012.

Archaeological Collections Management Practices in Middle Eastern Countries

Regional governments are exploring ways for better preserving their cultural heritage values because of the deterioration and destruction of archaeological sites and collections. Strategies driven by scientific study and the interpretation of the past based on the recovery, retrieval and interpretation of material evidence are actively being developed. The focus is on the potential of archaeological sites and collections to facilitate education, training, employment, research and tourism opportunities. Structured cooperation is needed between governments and archaeologists which aims to mitigate risks by managing changes, problems, issues and incidents emerging during the course of a project that may impact negatively on archaeological collections. A barrier to achieving this is current practice. Although an archaeological project has flexibility in what or if it chooses to document its systems, it should develop the amount of documentation it needs to demonstrate effective planning, operation, control and continual improvement of its management system and processes. This means systematically documenting all the processes involved in managing artefacts and collections. It includes, but is not limited to, recording procedures for in-field collecting, conservation and sampling, processing, washing, sorting and classification, registration, cataloguing, labelling and packing, post-excavation conservation, storage and curation, inventory control, data management, discard, and access and use.

Forward Planning

An archaeological collections management plan has been developed, based on study findings that incorporate strategic and integrated approaches to managing archaeological collections. It accounts for the legal and ethical requirements to which parties are subject. Its purpose is to provide a common definition of professional practice for local governments and archaeologists working in the Middle East. It is designed as a solution to assist cultural heritage professionals with strategies for sustainable long-term management and curation of archaeological collections excavated from research and salvage sites in the Middle East. It is distinct from, but can be integrated into, site management and conservation plans. It refers to current published standards, guidelines, protocols, charters and legislation found in Australian and international cultural heritage and research literature referenced in the bibliography. The application of this plan may be beneficial to existing projects with already well-developed management structures in place, or to assist in the development of new archaeological projects. Established sites may wish to improve or review their existing collections management procedures with a view to assessing whether current practices meet collections management good practice standards.

Recording Archaeological Collections

Archaeological sites may wish to utilise a plan to ensure that recovered archaeological collections will be managed and preserved by formalising and documenting existing management systems. An appropriate plan can be developed to formulate a long-term strategy and to provide clear future direction for the management of collections. The implementation of a plan for an existing site will necessitate an assessment of the existing condition of collections and a review of current site practices. Where an operational site has an existing site management plan there is potential for some overlap of information, however, this can be minimised if the information source is cross-referenced with existing policies and appropriate sections. For new archaeological projects a need exists to develop a theoretical basis for assessing the likely diversity and size of the collections that may be encountered. Adequate provisioning forms the basis of this approach. Short-term or salvage projects may produce a more comprehensive plan developed before the implementation stage, which takes into consideration the impact the project will have on all aspects of collections management, including cultural heritage status. The goal is to achieve reliable, sustainable and secure long-term management of research data and primary materials which constitute archaeological collections. The processes focus on managing sustainably physical, analogue (paper) and digital collections, chiefly by the necessity to document procedures which facilitate succession transitions and changes of key personnel during the lifetime of the project and after its completion. The aim is to present a framework with strategies that help ensure the long-term care and security of physical collections and, importantly, that facilitate access to consistent research data.

Management System for Collecting, Processing, Analysing and Curating

The study indicates that an archaeological collections management system should provide the framework of processes and procedures employed to ensure that the project can fulfill all tasks required to achieve its objectives.

General Requirements

Archaeological project directors can establish, document, implement and maintain a collections management system by adopting or adapting, in full or in part, the recommended activities by:

   a) Identifying the processes needed for the development of a management system and their application throughout the organisation.
   b) Determining the sequence and interaction of these processes.

c) Determining criteria and methods needed to ensure that both the operation and control of these processes are effective.
d) Ensuring the availability of resources and information necessary to support the operation and monitoring of these processes.
e) Monitoring and reviewing these processes for relevance and applicability.

Management Structure

An organisational structure is required that assigns specific responsibilities to appropriate personnel to undertake the range of activities required for managing archaeological collections, and ensuring that the aims of the archaeological collections management plan are met. To achieve this, archaeological project directors should appoint one or more personnel who, irrespective of other responsibilities, will form the core collection management team. This team will have the responsibility and authority for developing a sustainable material archive. The organisational structure defining the responsibilities should be kept current and reviewed on a regular basis, subject to the available resources.

Collections Management Responsibilities

The collections management team is responsible for managing the collections in an orderly and logical way, and to ensure their safe and secure custody. Key responsibilities include:

a) Ensuring that processes needed for the collections management system are established, implemented and maintained in accordance with documented policies.
b) Ensuring that collections are stored and packed so that they are protected from the environment, to prevent damage and limit degradation over time.

An archaeological registrar (or collections manager) will generally be responsible for collections inventory, tracking, and risk management, and should co-ordinate the overall planning for collections needs. The registrar and/or collections management team is responsible for cataloguing artefacts, the day-to-day care of collections, and collections access. They monitor storage conditions and conduct routine maintenance of collections in collaboration with the conservator and comply with local regulatory requirements. Other responsibilities include ensuring that all persons having contact with collections adhere to management policies for handling, packing and accessing. Guidance documents should be made available to relevant staff and responsibilities should be delegated for the control of each document. The role of the conservator is to care for the physical condition of archaeological collections. Assessing the condition of artefacts establishes whether there is a need for conservation and performing preventive or remedial conservation treatments. The conservator should also maintain and/or enhance the meaning and value of artefacts for the purposes of research and education.

Regulatory Responsibilities

Policies for managing archaeological collections should include steps to ensure compliance with local regulations. It should reference relevant legislation, standards ethical codes or international conventions and other departmental, political or external requirements that may affect managing archaeological collections. Procedures for liaising with local authorities should be documented.

Management Planning and System Review

A management review should outline measures to be taken before, during and after excavation in order to manage and protect archaeological collections. The effectiveness with which this can be done will depend on the resources allocated to on-site recording, processing and storage. The processes should ensure that:

a) Planning of the management system is carried out in order to meet the requirements, as well as ensuring the future needs of the project and site.
b) The integrity of the management system and its continued relevance is maintained when changes to the management system are planned and implemented.

The input into a management review should include information on:

An assessment of the performance and weaknesses of the system.

An assessment of the future direction of the project, its funding, regulatory changes, IT requirements, personnel changes and technology changes.

An assessment of the adequacy of site infrastructure, including storage, accommodation and equipment needs.

The output from the management review should include any decisions and actions related to:

a) An improvement of the effectiveness of the management system and its processes.
b) An assessment of future resource needs, both human resources and infrastructure.
c) Recommendations for improvement.

Documentation

A set of conventions for controlling the creation and use of framework documentation should be developed. A central index of all operational and policy documents should be maintained.

General

The management system documentation should include:

a) Documents needed by the project to ensure the effective planning, operation and control of its collections management processes.
b) Records required by this plan.

Operational Procedures

The operational procedures conducted for collecting, processing, cataloguing, accessing and further preparation of artefact collections, including long-term storage, should be documented in a series of approved and up-to-date procedural operating instructions. They should make clear the objectives and activities to be performed, the standards to be achieved and the desired outcomes. This documentation should include staff and resource requirements, implementation timetables as required and a process for monitoring progress. Operational procedures are listed:

a) Recording
b) Collecting and sampling
c) Registration and packing
d) Cleaning and washing
e) Sorting and classification
f) Cataloguing
g) Inventory
h) Labelling
i) Conservation
j) Photography and Illustration
k) Analysis
l) Materials Analysis
m) Classification
n) Data entry
o) Storage
p) Accessing

Control of Documents

Documentation created, distributed and retained for information and actions should be subject to a formal document control system. Records represent a special type of document and should be controlled according to the requirements given. Contents of controlled documents should be reviewed and updated on a regular basis, involving document users and receivers of the process; updated documents should be authorised as appropriate.[34] A documented procedure should be established to define the controls needed, such as:

a) Approving documents for adequacy prior to issue.
b) As necessary, the review, update and re-approval of documents.
c) Ensuring that changes and the current revision status of documents are identified.
d) Ensuring that relevant versions of applicable documents are available at points of use.
e) Ensuring that documents remain legible and readily identifiable.
f) Ensuring that documents of external origin are identified and their distribution controlled.
g) Preventing the unintended use of obsolete documents, and to apply suitable identification to them if they are retained for any purpose

File-naming strategies include:

- Version number
- Date of creation
- Name/initials of creator
- Description of content
- Name of research team/department associated with the data
- Publication date
- Project number
- File extension

Research data are described as:

- Data created in a digital form (born digital)
- Physical materials created or collected as part of the research process
- Analogue data stored in physical media (e.g. surface grooves of a vinyl record, the magnetic tape of a VCR cassette)
- Physical materials converted to a digital form (digitised)

Backup considerations:

- How will data be backed up?
- How often will full or incremental backup copies be made?
- How long will backups be stored?
- How much hard-drive space, or how many devices are needed to maintain backup schedule?
- How will different versions of data be tracked?
- Is a backup service used?

---

[34] University of Melbourne 2012. *Procedures and Guidelines for the Management of Research Data and Records*. http://researchdata.unimelb.edu.au/how(29/08/2015); see also EDINA, 2014. *MANTRA Research Data Management Training Modules 1, 6 and 8.* http://datalib.edina.ac.uk/mantra/ (29/08/2015).

- How is data secured?
- How are data files and identifying data destroyed at the end of a project?

Data preservation planning should include:

- Regular back up schedules (including multiple copies in multiple locations)
- Strategies to prevent data loss
- File format migration plans
- Check sums (bit integrity checking)
- Version control
- Data security
- Data storage media
- Copyright and licensing

Control of Records

Archaeological records refer to all written documentation and photographic material. They are interchangeable with documents and archives. Archaeological archives include any documentation related to an archaeological project, whether it is an excavation or survey project. Records should be established and maintained to provide evidence of conformity to requirements and of the effective operation of the management system. Records should remain legible, readily identifiable and retrievable. A documented procedure should be established to define the controls needed for the identification, storage, protection, retrieval, retention time and disposition of records. Actions should be taken to understand the properties of the media and to stabilise them in the best possible environment.

Resource Management

Resources and funding for archaeological sites can often be limited and require a significant level of prioritisation. Thus, resources for archaeological collections management should be efficiently and effectively deployed within these common limitations. A plan can better define all the requirements and facilitate the prioritisation of the resources for collection management.

Provision of Resources

It should be the policy of the archaeological project director to determine and provide the resources needed for:

a) Seeking an appropriate level of funding for managing archaeological collections into the future.
b) Implementing the management system and maintaining its effectiveness.
c) Providing, developing and supporting a diverse collections management team that will enable them to achieve the goals of the plan.

d) Adhering to both local and international regulations.
e) Ensuring the collections management team is responsible for artefacts and collections and has the authority to provision resources.

Human Resources

It should be the policy of the archaeological project director to ensure the employment of sufficient personnel with the necessary background, qualifications, training and experience to ensure that the requirements of the plan are met by:

a) Determining the necessary competence for personnel performing work affecting the management of the archaeological collections.
b) Providing training or taking other actions to satisfy these needs.
c) Evaluating the effectiveness of the training provided.
d) Ensuring that personnel are aware of the relevance and importance of their activities, and how they contribute to the achievement of the objectives of the plan.
e) Maintaining appropriate records of education, training, skills and experience.

Infrastructure

Archaeological project directors should determine, provide and maintain the infrastructure needed to achieve the objectives of the plan. Infrastructure includes:

a) Buildings, workspace and associated utilities
b) Process equipment (both hardware and software)
c) Supporting services (such as transport or communication)

Artefact Types and Characteristics

At some archaeological sites 'special finds' are recorded separately and individually into a database 'finds sheet'. Recorded information includes the unit number; a 'find number', its material type and artefact subgroup with a brief description. A unique system exists in Turkey whereby a governmental representative views special finds each day and assigns them as *etütlük* or *envanter. Etütlük* means that these artefacts are kept separately from all other materials so that they can be used as reference collections. These may or may not be accessioned into a museum. From an organisational perspective this means that artefacts from a season can be found in both general storage and in the reference collection. At the end of a season a list of all *etütlük* material is written and assigned individual numbers. *Envanter* means that at the end of a season these finds are accessioned into a museum. These artefacts are the most 'special' and most complete objects, and they are drawn and photographed. Each season new crates of *envanter* artefacts are created and recorded in the finds register. Each *envanter* artefact is securely packaged and boxed in consultation with conservators. Bulk finds are bagged and distributed to specialists for analyses, after which they are put into crates. Data is entered either directly into a finds register or recorded onto spreadsheets that list crate contents with area and unit numbers. The aim of maintaining a finds register is to produce accurate records and keep track of each artefact recovered, so as to provide information for the purpose of future study by specialists, researchers and students.

Collections Assessment

It is necessary to undertake an evaluation of the archaeological collections prior to the preparation of a plan. The plan needs to be sufficiently detailed to incorporate all information that may have an impact on the future management of the collections. New sites should develop predictive strategies to assess the future requirements of an effective plan.

Estimation of Collections Scope and Size for New Sites

Prior to implementation, new archaeological projects should make an assessment of the volume and types of archaeological collections which will need to be stored and of the raw materials required for packing, crating and, if necessary, shelving them. In addition, it should include an assessment of the amount of material that requires storage in particular environmental conditions. Thereafter, an additional estimate of space should be made for storage requirements specific to the anticipated duration of the project, as well as beyond project completion. Provisions should be made which stipulate the vision and objectives for managing archaeological collections on-site for short- (5 year), medium- (10 year) and long-term (25 years) periods, in agreement with stakeholders for resources such as adequately equipped storage buildings and laboratories, an interpretation centre or on-site museum, visitor facilities, protective fences and shelters.

Collections Scope and Size for Existing Sites

It is important for operational sites to establish the exact extent and nature of the stored archaeological collections. It is important to know the area of space that the collections currently occupy. An archaeological project should define the types of archaeological artefacts it collects in order to facilitate the development of a plan.

Description of Collections

Archaeological project directors should assess the size of the collections, describing the numbers and categories of artefacts, objects and special finds.

In addition to item quantities, the volume occupied needs to be recorded in overall cubic metres, numbers of crates, shelving, boxes, and any special storage facilities that may exist. Assessment of collections should also include associated documentary materials which provide contextual information integral for use in research and education. A description of the paper and digital records integral to the site and the mode of storage and access should be included in the assessment. Items requiring special attention, such as restoration or conservation treatments, should be itemised for adequate planning of future resource allocation.

Storage Crates, Boxes, Shelving Facilities

Archaeological project directors should ensure that a physical inspection of all significant groups or types of stored archaeological artefacts is done. The results should record both the number and types of storage containers in use for each category. The types and sizes of shelving, boxes, crates and custom made crates, needs to be assessed for planning purposes. The condition of existing containers should also be evaluated for both adequacy of purpose and damage to estimate the potential longevity of the items in use.

Condition of Archaeological Collections

A 'condition report' should be prepared that describes any deterioration in the collections, the plastic bags, labels, or other aspects of the condition that may be relevant to future planning.

Conservation and Preservation

A 'status report' should be prepared, detailing the conservation and preservation needs of an existing collection. Of key significance are the future requirements of the collection stored on-site and the level of backlogs that may exist for processing or studying any parts of the collection. Any special needs for parts of the collection should be described in order to facilitate future resourcing.

Storage Facilities

An evaluation of the adequacy of the existing storage facilities should be undertaken. This should include a prediction of the potential life of the facility to enable future storage needs to be predicted and provisioned adequately. A floor plan and storage layout can be utilised to assess the optimal use of space and the storage density of the site. Specific threats that may exist in the current facility should be identified and include an assessment of pest control, the potential for water damage and security risks.

Buildings: Shelters, Laboratories, Storage, Site Museum

An assessment of the condition should be made of all buildings and facilities that may impact on the status of the collections. This may be represented by temporary storage facilities in laboratories and conservation areas or local site museum. The use of alternative spaces may be impacted upon by specific work policies and particular study needs and thus these future requirements should also form part of the planning process for the site and the collections.

Collections Management

The care of archaeological collections should be managed, with concern for their long-term physical well-being and safety.

Collections Management Objectives

The care of archaeological collections should include issues of conservation, access and use, and inventory, as well as managing the overall composition of the collections in relation to the project's mission and goals.

Collections Management Policies

Collections management policies should be documented and contain specific details of what materials the project is going to collect in order to fulfil its mission and goals. The scope of collections should be defined and how these objectives will be achieved. The policies should consider the long-term research plans for the region.

Field Collection

Written field collection policy details should describe what will be collected during the archaeological fieldwork, how artefacts will be collected, and how they will be categorised and packed. The policy should provide guidance for the care of artefact classes and types that meet the collecting criteria of the project on the basis of their context, physical condition and relevance to the mission and objectives of the project. Projects developed by research institutions conduct their activities to enhance the understanding of the historic environment.

Salvage Excavation

Threat-led (salvage) projects respond to natural processes, proposed development, changes in agricultural land use or other events, offering a unique opportunity to study an historic asset. These projects are not generally research-driven. They are often funded by developers and conducted within strict time constraints. The need to collect as much data as possible before development begins can result in basic recording methods and loss of information. Activities can also be long-running projects undertaken by international universities in host countries.

Actions should be taken for preserving and storing finds from urgent and short-term excavations under threat by dam constructions, new roads and road improvement works, coal mining, other mining and housing projects. Archaeological collections management for salvage projects should aim to collect and document the maximum amount of data possible in order to prevent possible or present destruction. Data should be collected and recorded from a selected area within the nominated period and comply with local regulations.

Field Conservation And Preservation

Basic principles and methods of conservation should be practised on-site at all times. The likely kinds of material remains, the types of in-field conservation treatments, the volumes and kinds of archival-quality storage materials for transporting should all be anticipated, in addition to how material remains can be best collected to facilitate long-term preservation. The project should document guidance procedures for packing and storage artefacts according to appropriate standards.

Registration

The 'registrar' should have a written plan and procedures for post-excavation artefact registration which records primary data for artefact types and classes and identifies objects which may have exceptional historical, cultural, aesthetic, spiritual or scientific significance.

The registrar should:

a) Log in an artefact (or sample) and its associated data.
b) Assign, schedule, and track the artefact (or sample) and the associated analytical workload.
c) Implement processing and quality control associated with the artefact (or sample).
d) Store data associated with the artefact (or sample) analyses.
e) Inspect, approve, and compile artefact (or sample) data for reporting and/or further analysis, and create inventory lists which comply with local regulations.
f) The registration system should have the capability of achieving traceability of all items, related reports, and their location.

Laboratory Sampling and Management

Laboratory management systems should track and record the chain of custody and locations for artefacts (or samples).

Laboratory Conservation

The processes used for stabilising archaeological artefacts (or samples) should be recorded and stored in the documentary archive. Artefacts to be stored at local museums should be accompanied by copies of records containing this information and provide future recommendations for optimal storage in the museum.

Discard

A project intending to discard artefacts should develop a policy that defines what may or may not be discarded and under what circumstances and authorisation discard may occur. The discard policy should comply with local regulations. The project may choose to discard objects which do not meet the collecting criteria of the project on the basis of context, physical condition and relevance to the mission and objectives of the project, but representative samples of the discarded materials should be retained.

Cataloguing

The catalogue should record a complete inventory of artefacts present in the collection and facilitate the analytical goals of the project.

Labelling

Written guidelines should be produced setting out the information that is required to identify an artefact and how labels should be affixed, using the most permanent method applicable to its status, yet which is reversible.

Packing

The 'conservator' should produce written guidelines for the temporary packing of artefacts or for the actions to be taken until an artefact has been assessed, stabilised and prepared for permanent storage. Records should be kept in an environment which minimises deterioration.

Storage Environment

The storage environment should be of a spatial layout which best accommodates the types and numbers of materials in the archaeological collections to mitigate against risks and disasters. Permanent on-site storage facilities should be clean, organised and regularly checked throughout the year by a guard or other caretaker who can repair leaks and structural damage, eradicate pests and perform other maintenance. Monitoring sensitive materials and relative humidity in storage facilities should occur annually during the excavation season. A floor plan should be drawn to scale, which includes the dimensions between walls, showing a view from above of the relationships between spaces and other physical features and stored objects. Archaeological collections should be stored in facilities which are structurally sound and secure from theft. Access to archaeological collections should be limited to authorised personnel.

Conservation and Preservation

Conservation and preservation of archaeological artefacts and their associated records will be a continuing process with the goal of maintaining them in a stable condition. Interventive and preventive conservation of artefacts may be initiated:

    a) By routine procedures
    b) As part of the requirements of a specific project or enquiry
    c) By a request or order from an authorised person

Archaeological collections should be protected against fluctuations in relative humidity, extreme temperatures, flooding, fire, earthquakes, direct sunlight, rats, birds, other animals, mould, fungi, insects, dust and poor handling. Archaeological collections should be placed in labelled containers and stored above the ground.

Inventory

Artefact inventory lists should be furnished to government representatives that comply with local regulations.

Records and Data Management Systems

The 'registrar' should manage documents and records that are produced by the project as part of its archaeological operations for creating collections. The management system should include information on:

    a) Data to be generated and stored (digital and non-digital)
    b) Data types anticipated (file formats, volumes)
    c) Procedures used to collect data
    d) Procedures used to check data
    d) Procedures used for data verification
    e) Intellectual property, copyright and ownership
    f) Ethics, privacy and confidentiality requirements
    g) Safeguards and any environmental requirements
    h) Metadata standards

Data Storage and Retrieval System

Data are observations made on, and measurements taken from, artefacts that include contextual information. Data should be accurately recorded and manipulated in secure and accessible IT databases. A controlled vocabulary should be used for the consistent and efficient recording of relevant observations and measurements.

Paper Archive

Paper documents are permanent, valuable, non-current records of the project, with their original order and provenance intact, which were created the by the project.

Publications

A publication may be defined as information distributed through communications media including:

a) Books (monographs, biographies, reference works, bound collection catalogues, exhibition catalogues and similar works)
b) Articles in journals or newspapers
c) Pamphlets (site bulletins, fliers, brochures, or special handouts)
d) Archival finding aids such as indices, Internet databases, or folder lists
e) Motion picture films, filmstrips, and commercial programmatic video tapes
f) Sound recordings
g) Research reports
h) Published slide-show packages and mass-distributed portfolios of prints and photographs
i) CD-ROMs containing software, games, and virtual museum tours
j) Internet sites

Electronic, Film and Photographic Archives

The composition and physical structure of electronic, film and photographic archives should be preserved for long-term care by:

a) Storing in adequate environmental conditions
b) Storing in proper storage enclosures
c) Careful handling practices

Access and Use of Collections

The 'registrar' should authorise and provide physical access to artefact collections in storage. Processes should be established for interested stakeholders to gain intellectual access through the available documentation and background data on the objects through IT databases and websites. These include:

    a) Annual excavation records
    b) Analyses records
    c) Photographs
    d) Publications
    e) Site diaries

Short-Term: Registration, Analysis And Access

Archaeologists, conservators and curators share common concerns about funding, storage and the general lack of policies. Additional concerns relate to planning, documentation and information systems, and access to archaeological collections. Specific concerns relate to staff wages, local government fees, resources and supplies, equipment and training costs. A lack of on-site policies for managing archaeological collections from their own professional perspectives, and from the perspective of local governmental requirements, was also expressed. A high percentage of archaeologists employ 'quality' principles when executing the phases of their projects. However, current approaches for managing archaeological collections tend to lack scope, formality and standardisation. Standard requirements suggest these issues would best be dealt with in the pre-excavation project design phase. The study found that the same basic archaeological process outlined in the English and Dutch models is practised widely by research and salvage projects in the Middle East. The main differences were the timelines, reporting content and the archaeological collections management requirements. Collecting and discard were two main areas which require clarification. A collections management system is needed that solves on-site storage and backlog problems and yet organise new and in-coming collections.

The Collections Management System

Formalised site policies and procedures are necessary for familiarising all personnel and directorate staff with on-site archaeological collections management practice. Improved strategies for a sustainable collections management system are suggested because the study signified that only 57% of archaeological projects provide written training manuals for site personnel, students and/or volunteers, and only 45% arrange long-term care with museums in the planning phase. This is further supported by changing legislation, regulations and codes of practice. Well-written site policies are statements of principles and practice that reflect the ongoing management and administration of a project.

Policies and Procedures

Policies and procedures should be developed that reflect the ownership of intellectual property rights of archaeological collections, which should cover the following issues:

    a) The purpose of giving researchers copies
    b) Procedures for obtaining copies
    c) Procedures for requesting and obtaining publishing permissions, rights clearances and licences

d) Acknowledgement procedures
e) How and when logos and names should be used
f) Pre-publication review procedures

Loans

A project intending to loan objects or collections should establish a policy that defines the conditions under which any site materials are loaned or temporarily removed from the site. Processes should be established which comply with the objectives of the project and local regulations.

Researcher Access

The 'registrar' should issue written procedures and guidelines for accessing and specifying the proper handling of archaeological materials in accordance with the project's objectives and goals.

Destructive Analysis

Archaeological project directors should ensure that the purpose for legitimate destructive or scientific analysis is clearly documented in the research design and complies with local regulations.

Legal

This policy should document and describe the measures in place to meet any special conditions set out by local regulations, such as the export of artefacts or samples.

Inventory Management

A policy should be developed for the maintenance of up-to-date information accounting for and locating all archaeological objects and collections for which it is legally responsible. This includes objects or collections on loan, previously undocumented or temporarily deposited off-site. The procedure for inventory control should:

a) Enable accountability for any object or collection at any time
b) Enable the provision of up-to-date information about all objects or collections in the care of the project
c) Provide the current location of each object or collection

Annual Inventory of Collections

A full inventory of all on-site bulk collections and a random sample inventory of all catalogued collections should be conducted annually. This should include the physical location, condition and documentation for objects in the collection.

Object Locations

Object locations should be catalogued to maintain locational information for all objects and collections. This should include an inventory of all objects stored at local or regional museums.

Collections Annual Report

A policy should be established for annual inventory reporting.

Collections Significance Criteria

An overarching statement of cultural significance should be a concise interpretation of the historic, cultural, aesthetic, spiritual or scientific values of an object or a collection(s) in the context of the site from where it/they were excavated. A statement of cultural significance may be used in support of applications for funding, heritage listing and site management and conservation. A statement of cultural significance identifying one or more of the above primary criteria would be useful to local museums when accessioning selected artefacts from inventory lists at the end of the excavation season. The scientific significance of archaeological collections can be determined by the scope, quality and quantity of records containing data about observations, measurements, analysis and the interpretation of artefacts (or samples) by archaeological specialists. Research significance may be determined by the ability of data records to answer contemporary research questions, in addition to their accuracy, validity, accessibility and security.

Security and Succession Planning

The employment (and wages) for both off- and on-site security personnel is the organising and financial responsibility of the project director. Archaeological project directors should establish a succession plan and a process for identifying and developing internal personnel with the potential to assume full leadership of the project, and which complies with local legal requirements. A procedure should be developed for transferring a full site archive to the host country.

Emergency Planning/Disaster Response

A 'disaster plan' should be established to ensure damage limitation in the event of a disaster. The general contents of the plan should be made known to all staff and volunteers through prior discussion, regular training sessions and emergency exercises. An adequate plan should enable a new or unplanned directorship to assume responsibility for collections and understand the full organisational and operational status thereof.

Threats to Archaeological Collections

Archaeological project directors are responsible for the hiring of guards and for the security of the storage depots. A risk management plan should be developed with policies and procedures for dealing with risks to the archaeological collections, such as fire, flooding, pests, accidental damage, theft, vandalism and other disasters. Its general contents should be made known to all staff and volunteers through prior discussion, regular training sessions and emergency exercises.

Threats to Documentary Archive

Archaeological project directors should establish a policy and procedures for mitigating risks to the documentary archive, such as fire, flood, pests, accidental damage, theft, vandalism and other disasters. Its general contents should be made known to all staff and volunteers through prior discussion, regular training sessions and emergency exercises.

Role of Registrars

Registrars organise and gather information about artefact classes, types and numbers. The aim of having an on-site registrar, or collections manager, is to manage the 'finds' system. The system develops a sustainable material archive for current and future research and produces artefacts and collections. Strategies for managing artefacts coming in from the field may include undergoing an initial condition assessment and cleaning, followed by sorting, registration and cataloguing. They record, document and archive contextual information about artefacts and links to excavators and specialists. In addition to keeping track of post-recovery movements of artefacts, registrars decide how and where artefacts will be stored in the short term. Figure 8 provides an example of the 'object' triage process employed at Tell Ta'yinat for assigning significance, identifying condition and conservation issues, classifying and storing.[35]

Registrars are also responsible for the security of the 'finds laboratory.' They must ensure that all finds are brought straight to the finds laboratory from the site at the end of each day. As recovered, all finds should be put into a bucket or container and remain in that container until handed over to the registrar. In the absence of the registrar, finds laboratories should remain locked if unattended. Sign-out sheets are used at some large sites if artefacts or crates are removed for study purposes.

---

[35] Adapted from Tell Ta'yinat triage system 2012.

Short-Term: Registration, Analysis And Access

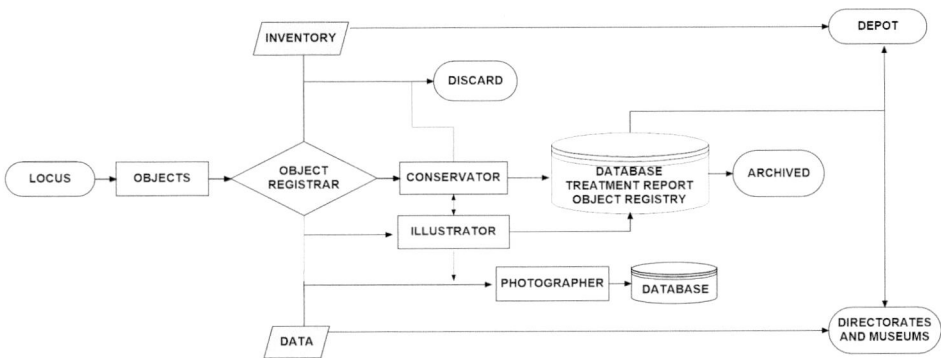

FIGURE 8: TELL TA'YINAT 'OBJECT' TRIAGE PROCESS.

Role of Conservators

Long-term storage requires the continued stabilisation of artefacts through the life of the project. Conserving artefacts is integral to the archaeological process. At some sites registrars and conservators are central to this process. Conservators may assist archaeologists in establishing the conservation needs and priorities of a project. Assistance may be provided for determining and implementing policies and procedures for the safe recovery, recording and processing of all archaeological materials. Once artefacts are stabilised conservators may be required to ensure that handling, studying and storage do not impede stability. Artefacts must be stored and packaged so that they are protected from the environment, so that damage is prevented and degradation over time is limited. The usefulness of an artefact as an interpretive tool is dependent upon its storage conditions. All artefacts stored on-site should be cared for according to good and practical museum standards. Continual condition assessment of all artefacts is required on a regular basis, as is close co-operation with on-site conservators. These actions ensure the continued stabilisation of artefacts throughout the life period of an archaeological project. Preventive techniques play a vital role in protecting archaeological materials.[36]

Role of Archaeological Specialists

Collections can be created by archaeological missions undertaking basic research, applied research or development projects. The study indicated that specialists at 93% of sites identify work needing to be carried out. At some sites this includes making recommendations, developing and implementing research programs and interpretation of archaeology for visitors. Specialists relate archaeological findings to historical documentation and provide reports on excavation

---

[36] Willems and Brandt 2004, 59; see also Sease 1999, 2.

activities and analyses of collections. In addition, specialists prepare and present archaeological information for various groups and maintain records and prepare correspondence related to their work. In some cases after specialist analysis, finds and samples are packed, coded and registered with the corresponding archive in accordance with the project's policy before being transferred to the museum or storage depot.

Assessing Significance

After artefacts have been processed they are subject to a number of assessments. Although for long-term preservation purposes artefacts are assessed on their physical condition, they are also evaluated for their future research potential. A formal method with specific evaluative criteria for assessing the significance of the values of 'a place', for instance that recommended in the Burra Charter, was employed by case study site No. 3. The method was used to produce a 'statement of significance' identifying the site's cultural, aesthetic, historical, scientific and educational values in the site management plan.[37] According to this method, the study found that all of the case study sites were culturally significant and possessed all of those values in varying degrees. However, this method does not provide guidance for assessing the significance of artefacts or archaeological collections for recovery or investigative processes. Rather, the project collecting policy determines what artefacts will be kept for further research and what artefacts will be discarded. The material types and characteristics of artefacts were determining factors on which the initial research potential and significance at a quantifiable level were based. Primary and secondary data which confirmed the legitimate characteristics of artefacts capable of answering the research questions were additional determining factors, as were the strategies that were executed for managing and preserving both artefacts and data. The study found that 40% of archaeological collections stored at sites demonstrated greater diversity in types than the remaining 60%, which consisted of two classes of artefacts, namely, ceramics and bone. Museum objects constitute less than 1% of the overall archaeological collections.

Survey participants rated alternative criteria, 'context, datability, rarity, condition, diversity and site significance' for their usefulness in deciding what artefacts or parts of the collection were to be saved for long-term care.[38] These criteria more accurately reflect investigative phases within the archaeological process. The ratings for each criterion show a diversity of opinions, as seen in Figure 9.

---

[37] Çatalhöyük Site Management Plan 2004, 7; see also Australia ICOMOS Burra Charter 2014; 2013; 2004; 1999.
[38] Archaeologists, conservators and curators rated the alternative criteria as 10 = very important; 1 = not important.

Significance Criteria	Archaeologists	Conservators	Curators
Condition	5	4	6
Context	1	2	1
Datability	3	3	4
Diversity	4	5	5
Rarity	4	1	3
Site Significance	2	6	2

FIGURE 9: MOST TO LEAST 'USEFUL' RATING.

Studying and understanding the meaning and values of artefacts and collections is a process achieved by analyses, understanding the history and context and identifying the value for communities. In the first instance archaeologists create data which are facts and/or observations on which their argument, theory or test is based. Research data relates to contemporary research trends and should be relevant. Its value could be high, medium or low and may be used for informing national heritage registers, significance assessments, site management plans, conservation plans and/or funding applications. It may also be used to inform decisions to discard redundant artefacts or collections. In the broadest sense, scientific significance is the value placed on material by the scientific community. The archaeological community may regard artefacts or archaeological samples as having great scientific value but these may have no value at all outside the framework of the investigation. Material which is integrated into the fabric of science, and material which facilitates scientific work are the main categories which have traditionally been regarded as having scientific value. Since archaeological artefacts and collections are values of a site, their further research potential is determined by accurately documented contextual references, dating and associated data. Their frequency, diversity or condition when compared proportionately to all other artefacts also helps determine their potential for further research. Scientific data created as a result of analysing a range of characteristics and relationships are interpreted by specialists whose narratives form the basis of further local, regional, national and international research initiatives. Only once archaeological artefacts and collections have endured and survived the archaeological process, can other narratives be constructed about their cultural significance or aesthetic, historic, scientific, social or spiritual values for past, present or future generations.[39] A conservation-led model designed for preserving museum archaeological collections suggests that a plan to manage them sustainably into the future should aim for permanent and secure dry storage for a period of 100 years as the ultimate goal.[40]

---

[39] Australia ICOMOS Burra Charter 2013, 2. Article 1.
[40] Waller 2014, 11.

Access to On-Site Collections

Datasets are studied by numerous on-site specialists and some specialists need to access multiple datasets. For this reason, it is necessary for the registrar to know exactly where all registered artefacts are at all times. Artefacts or crates of artefacts that are removed from the immediate care of the registrar should be signed out. This prevents time lost in looking for an artefact (or crate of artefacts) if already removed. When an artefact is moved, or if a crate is re-arranged, registrars should be notified of the changes so that the location database can be updated. This is an important procedure and part of legally required security. This reduces the risks of artefacts, or crates of artefacts, being misplaced and assists specialists, students and the registrar in being able to locate artefacts easily. Ordering systems established by registrars and/or specialists should be observed as a matter of professional courtesy.[41]

---

[41] Cassidy and Guerre 2009, 5. Çatalhöyük Finds Guidance.

Long-Term: Archaeological Collections Storage

Standard for Storing and Curating On-Site Archaeological Collections

International Charters and Conventions

Early in the 20th century the international community began to initiate preservation solutions because of the illegal trade in antiquities, disputes over ownership, unauthorised excavations, and destruction of sites.[42] In 1940, under the auspices of the International Committee of Intellectual Co-operation (ICIC) an advisory body to the League of Nations (LN), the International Museums Office (IMO) published the 'Manual on the Technique of Archaeological Excavation'.[43] This early standardisation contains guidance and advice on surveying methods, organising excavations and technical methodologies. It recommends methods for recording, equipment use, conserving artefacts and site preservation. These basic principles depend on the nature of an excavation, the state of preservation of artefacts and the periods represented.[44]

United Nations Educational and Scientific Organisation (UNESCO)

Not long after this standard was published the United Nations (UN) was formed in 1945, replacing the League of Nations (LN) immediately after WWII. In the same year the UN created UNESCO, a specialised agency to promote international collaboration through education, science and culture. The 1956 Recommendation on International Principles Applicable to Archaeological Excavations alludes to archaeological collections management practices.[45] It declared that artefacts discovered as a result of archaeological excavation should be protected because their preservation was in the public interest from the point of view of history or art and architecture.[46] This recommendation compelled excavators to declare movable or immovable objects of archaeological character which may be discovered and to employ minimum standards to protect archaeological heritage, although procedures are not specified.[47]

---

[42] Albright 1923; see also Iraq Museum 2013; Israeli Antiquities Authority 2011; Boast 2009; 2002; 165; Kantner 2008, 37; Trigger 2007, 215; Alexandri 2002, 19; Boast 2002, 291; Kaeser 2002, 170; Murray 2002, 235; Nordbladh 2002; Fagan 1995, 1; Kirk 1946; International Institute of Intellectual Co-Operation 1940; Fisher 1925, 16.
[43] International Museums Office 1940. *Manual on the Technique of Archaeological Excavations*; see also Hall 2011, 2.
[44] International Museums Office 1940, 172.
[45] UNESCO 1956, 41–44.
[46] UNESCO 1956, 41. Archaeological excavation is defined as any research aimed at the discovery of objects of archaeological character, whether such research involves digging of the ground or systematic exploration of its surface or is carried out on the bed or in the subsoil of inland or territorial waters of a Member State.
[47] UNESCO 1956, 41–42. Principles recommended by UNESCO to protect archaeological heritage are:
  a) Make archaeological explorations and excavations subject to prior authorisation by the competent authority.
  b) Oblige any person finding archaeological remains to declare them at the earliest possible date to the

Further endorsed was the organisation of national antiquities departments or 'directorates' which are responsible for overseeing archaeological excavations and which can undertake emergency archaeological work itself. Signatories are advised to establish a central documentation repository.[48] Co-operation with research institutes and universities for technical training of excavators is recommended, as are efforts to obtain adequate funding.[49] Careful supervision for granting permits and for restoration of archaeological remains and objects is sanctioned.[50] Signatories to the Convention Concerning the Protection of the World Cultural and Natural Heritage (1972) pledge to adopt policies which help protect, conserve and present cultural heritage and administer those initiatives using legal and scientific means.[51] Other charters, protocols and recommendations are primarily concerned with preservation initiatives and prohibiting illicit import, export and theft of cultural property. By signing a convention each country pledges to conserve not only World Heritage sites but also to protect its own national heritage. An agreement involves providing details of how a property is protected and provides a management plan for its upkeep. Members are expected to protect the World Heritage values of properties and to provide condition reports.[52] The World Heritage Convention defines the duties of members in identifying potential sites and requirements for protecting and preserving them.[53] However,

---

competent authority.
c) Impose penalties for the infringement of these regulations.
d) Make undeclared objects subject to confiscation.
e) Define the legal status of the archaeological sub-soil and, where State ownership of the said sub-soil is recognised, specifically mention the fact in its legislation.
f) Consider classifying as historical monuments the essential elements of its archaeological heritage.

[48] UNESCO 1956, 42. The central documentation registry should include maps of locations where movable and immovable monuments were/are located and additional documentation for every important museum or ceramic, or iconographic collections.

[49] UNESCO 1956. Steps should be taken to ensure regular provision of funds to administer the services in a satisfactory manner; to carry out a program of work proportionate to the archaeological resources of the country, including scientific publications; to exercise control over accidental discoveries; and to provide for the upkeep of excavation sites and monuments.

[50] UNESCO 1956, 2-3. Prior approval should be obtained from the competent authority before any monuments are removed which ought to remain *in situ*.

[51] UNESCO 1972, 2-3. Article 1. Cultural heritage is defined as having three main categories. These are monuments, groups of buildings and sites. Monuments are defined as architectural works, works of monumental sculpture and painting, elements or structures of an archaeological nature, inscriptions, cave dwellings and combinations of features, which are of outstanding universal value from the point of view of history, art or science. Groups of buildings are defined as groups of separate or connected buildings which, because of their architecture, their homogeneity or their place in the landscape, are of outstanding universal value from the point of view of history, art or science. Sites are defined as works of man or the combined works of nature and man, and areas including archaeological sites which are of outstanding universal value from the historical, aesthetic, ethnological or anthropological point of view.

[52] UNESCO 2013. *State Parties*. http://whc.unesco.org/en/statesparties (07/12/2013). In addition to a number of other criteria, this is done by integrating measures for protection of cultural and natural heritage into regional planning programs and undertaking scientific and technical conservation research. State Parties are countries which have ratified the World Heritage Convention. In essence, State Parties agree to identify and nominate properties on their national territory to be considered for inscription on the World Heritage List.

[53] UNESCO 2013. *Charters and Conventions*. http://whc.unesco.org/en/convention/ (07/12/2013). The idea of creating an international movement for protecting heritage emerged after World War I. The 1972 Convention concerning the Protection of the World Cultural and Natural Heritage developed from the merging of two

by comparison tentative and/or listed World Heritage sites represent a very small percentage of archaeological sites being excavated in signatory countries.

International Centre for the Study of the Preservation and Restoration of Cultural Property (ICCROM)

In 1956 ICCROM was created by UNESCO. This body was created to study and improve restoration methods.[54] It is a multidisciplinary training institution which participates in collaborative efforts for conservation. It involves scientists, conservators, restorers, archaeologists, art historians, curators, architects, engineers and city planners. ICCROM members are individual states which have declared their adhesion to these principles. In 2010 to assist museums in developing countries ICCROM with UNESCO produced guidance documents which focus on documentation of museum collections; risk and deterioration assessment for preventive conservation; preventive conservation for collections in store and integrated emergency management.[55]

International Council on Monuments and Sites (ICOMOS)

ICOMOS was created in 1964 and works toward conserving and protecting significant cultural heritage 'places.' It promotes the application of theory, methodology, and scientific techniques for conserving architectural and archaeological heritage.[56] ICOMOS advises signatories to UNESCO's 1972 Convention Concerning the Protection of the World Cultural and Natural Heritage World Heritage.[57] Signatories who adopt this convention agree that their duty is to ensure that listed and tentative properties are identified, protected, conserved and presented for future generations. This charter declares that the protection of heritage cannot be based on the application of archaeological techniques alone.[58] Article 2 recommends that archaeological heritage should be integrated

---

separate movements: the first focusing on the preservation of cultural sites, and the other dealing with the conservation of nature.

[54] ICCROM 2009. *Brief History*. Website: http://www.iccrom.org/eng/00about_en/00_03history_en.shtml (05/03/2014).

[55] ICCROM 2010. UNESCO-ICCROM Partnership for the Preventive Conservation of Endangered Museum Collections in Developing countries (2007-2010). Website: http://www.unesco.org/new/en/culture/themes/museums/unescoiccrom-re-org/unesco-iccrom-partnership-for-the-preventive-conservation-of-endangered-museum-collections-in-developing-countries-2007-2010/(15/08/2016); see also RE-ORG. Tools for Storage Reorganisation and Documentation System. Website: http://www.unesco.org/new/en/culture/themes/museums/unescoiccrom-re-org/unesco-iccrom-partnership-for-the-preventive-conservation-of-endangered-museum-collections-in-developing-countries-2007-2010/(15/08/2016).

[56] ICOMOS 2011. International Council on Monuments and Sites. Website: http://www.icomos.org/en/about-icomos/mission-and-vision/statutes-and-policies (16/12/13).

[57] ICOMOS 2014. *Managing Cultural World Heritage*. Website: http://openarchive.icomos.org/1465/ (07/03/2014).

[58] ICOMOS-ICAHM 1990. *Charter for the Protection and Management of the Archaeological Heritage*. Defines archaeological heritage as that part of the material heritage in respect of which archaeological methods provide primary information. It comprises all vestiges of human existence and consists of places relating to all manifestations of human activity, abandoned structures, and remains of all kinds (including subterranean and

into planning policies at international, national, regional and local levels. The measures it recommends for protecting archaeological heritage relate to survey, investigation, maintenance and conservation; presentation, information and reconstruction; professional qualifications and international co-operation. The recommendations cite UNESCO's 1956 Recommendations on International Principles Applicable to Archaeological Excavations. The International Scientific Committee on Archaeological Heritage Management (ICAHM) advises ICOMOS and the World Heritage Committee on various aspects concerning the management of archaeological sites and landscapes with regard to tangible and intangible cultural heritage.[59] The recommendations are based on existing UNESCO conventions.[60]

One of ICAHM's functions is to formulate standards and practices for both archaeological research and for Cultural Resource Management (CRM).[61] The 1990 Charter for the Protection and Management of the Archaeological Heritage expands on UNESCO's 1956 convention by including principles for professional performance of the processes of listing, survey, excavation, documentation, research, maintenance, conservation, preservation, reconstruction, information, presentation, public access and use of the heritage, and the qualification of professionals involved in the protection of the archaeological heritage.[62] Draft guidelines for the Charter for the Protection and Management of the Archaeological Heritage created in July 2010 reiterate the overarching themes for preserving archaeological heritage places, but do not contain specific reference to or advice on how archaeological collections should be managed in general or on those stored at archaeological sites.[63]

---

underwater sites), together with all the portable cultural material associated with them.

[59] ICAHM 2009. Website: http://www.icomos.org/icahm/index.html(14/03/2014); see also ICOMOS/ICAHM 2010, 518. Intangible cultural heritage constitutes part of the living traditions of indigenous peoples. The *1999 International Cultural Tourism Charter* was adopted in 2010 (01/08/2015).

[60] ICAHM 2009. Website: http://www.icomos.org/icahm/index.html (14/03/2014).

[61] Davis 1972, 267; see also Kerber 1994, 2. Cultural Resource Management began in the United States in the 1960s and 1970s in response to the curation crisis in museums and repositories which occurred as a result of new regulations, the 1990 Curation of Federally Owned and Administered Archaeological Collections Act (36CFR79). CRM is defined as tangible and intangible aspects of cultural systems, both living and dead, that are valued by or representative of a given culture or that contain information about a culture. It includes but is not limited to sites, structures, districts, objects and historic documents associated with or representative of peoples, cultures, and human activities and events, either in the present or in the past. Cultural resources also can include the primary written and verbal data for interpretation and understanding of those tangible resources.

[62] The measures it recommends for protecting archaeological heritage relate to survey; investigation; maintenance and conservation; presentation, information and reconstruction; professional qualifications and international co-operation.

[63] ICOMOS/ICAHM 2010. *Draft Guidelines for the Charter for the Protection and Management of the Archaeological Heritage*. It recommends that archaeological heritage should be integrated into planning policies at international, national, regional and local levels. The measures it recommends for protecting archaeological heritage relate to survey; investigation; maintenance and conservation; presentation, information and reconstruction; professional qualifications and international co-operation.

In 2013 Australia ICOMOS conducted a review of *The Burra Charter* 1999 with its amendments. The Charter is an internationally accepted standard for managing cultural heritage places that was first adopted by Australia ICOMOS in 1979.[64] Its most recent update reflects current theory and practice for assessing and managing cultural heritage places. The standard includes a series of 'practice notes' that provide a method for assessing the cultural significance of artefacts and places. It aims to assist archaeologists and heritage professionals in preparing overarching 'statements of significance' that interpret the significance of a 'place' or archaeological site.[65] This model assesses archaeological artefacts and/or collections on their culturally significant 'values'.[66]

International Council of Museums (ICOM)

In 1946 the International Council of Museums (ICOM) was created. Guidelines for managing museum archaeological collections were produced before and after ICOM's adoption of a Code of Ethics for Museums in 1986.[67] This code and other guidelines for managing archaeological collections are used by the international museum community.[68] ICOM aims to create minimum standards and guidelines, many of which are multilingual, for professional practices for museums and museum employees.[69] ICOM established an international advisory committee, the International Committee for Documentation (CIDOC), to provide the museum community with advice on good practice. CIDOC is dedicated to documenting museum collections. The committee consists of curators, librarians and specialists in documentation, registration, collections management and computerisation. Members participate in creating data standards for both general and specific aspects of cultural heritage, multimedia and/or the Internet.[70] Figure 10 provides an example of ICOM/CIDOC museum standards and guidelines relating to archaeological collections.[71]

---

[64] Australia ICOMOS 1999, *The Burra Charter*. Website: http://australia.icomos.org/publications/charters/ (12/08/2015); see also Australian Government 2014, 9-12. *Guidelines for Expert Examiners under the Protection of Movable Cultural Heritage Act 1986;* Deeben *et al.* 1999, 177; see also Greene 1999, 43; Trigger 1984, 355; Tainter and Lucas 1983, 707; Clark 1982, 217; Bowdler 1981, 123; Lynott 1980, 117; Moratto and Kelly 1978, 1; Raab and Klinger 1977, 629.

[65] *The Burra Charter and Archaeological Practice* 2013. http://australia.icomos.org/wp-content/uploads/Practice-Note_The-Burra-Charter-and-Archaeological-Practice.pdf (12/08/2015).

[66] *The Burra Charter 1999*, Article 1, 1.2. Cultural significance means aesthetic, historic, scientific, social or spiritual value for past, present or future generations. It is embodied in the place itself, its fabric, setting, use, associations, meanings, records, related places and related objects.

[67] ICOM 1986 *Code of Ethics for Museums*. Website: http://www.iccrom.org/eng/00about_en.shtml (16/12/13). Formerly International Museums Office (IMO) established in 1940; see also Braunholtz 1953, 109; De Beer 1953, 3.

[68] ICOM 2012.*Organisation*. Website: http://icom.museum/the-organisation/icom-missions/ (16/12/13).

[69] ICOM 2007. *Running a Museum: A Practical Handbook*. Available in English, Arabic and French.

[70] CIDOC 2015. *International Committee for Documentation*. Website: http://icom.museum/the-committees/international-committees/international-committee/international-committee-for-documentation/ (01/08/2015).

[71] ICOM 2012. *Standards and guidelines*. Website: http://icom.museum/professional-standards/standards-guidelines/ (06/03/2014).

ICOM/CIDOC Standards and Guidelines	
2004	Running a Museum: a practical handbook
1995	Recommendations for the Application of Accession Numbers
1995	CIDOC Fact Sheet No. 1. Registration Step by Step: When an Object Enters the Museum
1995	International Guidelines for Museum Object Information: the CIDOC Information Categories
1993	CIDOC Fact Sheet No. 2. Labelling and Marking Objects
1993	Guidelines for Disaster Preparedness in Museums
1992	Draft International Core Data Standard for Archaeological Sites and Monuments

FIGURE 10: ICOM/CIDOC STANDARDS AND GUIDELINES.

Archaeological Site Management and Conservation

Managing and conserving archaeological sites has become increasingly important since the 1950s. International guidelines have been produced for preparing site management and site conservation plans specifically to help document, protect and value archaeological sites and heritage. However, the overall objective is to control and develop land use, to minimise the destruction of 'archaeological heritage' and to preserve monuments and sites *in situ*. In more recent times planning processes have come to include educational activities, community involvement, and visitor management, but do not include strategies for managing excavated archaeological collections. Solutions for evaluating future preservation and storage needs of collections relate to museum collections and storerooms but not for on-site archaeological facilities. Although guidance exists for conservators working on archaeological sites, the main problems which have not been addressed by legislation, charters, protocols and recommendations are those of long-term preservation and the housing of vast amounts of artefacts recovered through archaeological survey and excavations.[72] These guides provide information about on-site conservation activities and stabilising excavated materials.

Estimating Storage Provision and Future Expansion Needs

Defining storage space requirements is complicated as it involves extrapolating into physical space factors that are difficult to quantify, such as projected growth, requirements for access and use, and preventive conservation.[73] Another

---

[72] Pedeli and Pulga 2013; see also Kariya and Nielsen 2002, 4-5; Özen and Spirydowicz 2002, 4; Roth and Tsu 2002, 5; Severson and Ersoy 2002, 3; Spirydowicz 2002, 5; Spirydowicz and Özen 2002, 4; Strahan and Unruh 2002, 5; Wharton and Ersoy 2002, 4; Stanley-Price 1995; Dollery 1994, 71.

[73] Lambert and Mottus 2014, 1-2. Six published methods for calculating space used by museums were tested by the authors on a storage area (41m^2); a) Basic order-of-magnitude; b) Guesstimating storage space; c) RE-

difficulty is that archaeological sites are often compelled to make use of unused rooms in private dwellings, ex-government or farm buildings, or spaces already located on or near their sites. Likewise, it is hard to know accurately the numbers of containers that hold artefacts stored on-site and the actual space that the containers occupy. On-site needs can be understood more clearly by analysing the study data. The study found that an average 1300kg of archaeological material is recovered each year by each archaeological project and that the average project duration is 23.5 years. The study found case study sites recover 1016kg of archaeological material each year and that the average duration for these projects is 16.6 years. The combined averaged findings suggest that 1160kg, or 78 crates, of archaeological material are excavated per annum and that projects run for 20 years.[74] As a basis for calculations, 4.8m^2 is used as the lowest annual square metre increase and 98m^2 should be regarded as a *minimum* space requirement over the life of a long-term project (Figure 11). However, these calculations depend on being able to establish the duration of a project, the type of storage containers, fixtures and the building configuration.

International standards indicate that records created as a result of the process(s) should be based on standard documentary and management systems that incorporate procedures required for the physical aspects of on-site storage. A structured planning approach which articulates the research potential and significance of a site incorporates the whole archaeological process and should extend to managing archaeological collections. The study found there is a general absence of standardisation for maintaining recovery records, specifications for cataloguing and inventory lists, specifications for descriptive information about artefacts and/or collections, specifications for photographs/images, locational information, condition information, and for monitoring records on discard. Implementing standards for protecting physical collections requires an adequate

On-site storage space projection	Kg per annum	Crates per annum (15kg per crate)	Project duration (years)	Project duration (crates)	Annual sqm increment (16 crates per m^2)	Project duration (m^2 space)
Surveys (*n*=32)	1300	87	23.5	2044	5.4	128
Field-study (*n*=5)	1020	68	16.6	1129	4.3	71
Average	1160	78	20.1	1568	4.8	98

FIGURE 11: ON-SITE STORAGE SPACE PROJECTION.

ORG; d) US National Park Service Conserve O Grams; e) Estimating space for ethnographic collections, and f) Detailed calculation method. The authors found all methods to be insufficient.

[74] This was achieved by optimising floor space at 16 crates per square metre, estimating 15kg maximum per crate and allowing 1.5m corridors for walkways.

budget and detailed specifications for equipment and spaces for storage, study and conservation. Written specifications are needed for handling, storing, cleaning, conserving and organising collections that are appropriate to the nature of the materials and that protect objects and preserve data. Additional specifications for storing forms and records in a protected manner are required, as are specifications for regular inspection of collections, conducting inventories and for providing access to on-site collections for researchers. Documents which outline policies and describe procedures for handling, storing, cleaning, conserving and organising collections appropriate to the nature of the materials which protect objects and preserve data are necessary. Added to these requirements is the need for specifications for maintaining recovery records, catalogues and inventory lists; likewise for photographs/images, locational information, condition information and monitoring records on lost or damaged objects or records on discard. Adequate planning necessitates regular inspection of collections, conducting inventories and providing access to on-site collections for specialists, researchers and students. To achieve this, policies are required that relate to on-site safety, security for limited access and for periodic inspections of collections. Policies are also required for storing forms and records in a protected manner, for the physical security of collections to mitigate risks of fire, intrusion and emergency, and for building standards for storage depots at archaeological sites.

On-Site Storage Facilities for Archaeological Collections

Archaeological activities create physical masses of archaeological material that need to be cared for into the future. However, many funding bodies do not grant capital expenditure for constructing storage depots or for building on-site museums and many archaeologists cannot and do not accurately predict their long-term requirements. In the past, this cost has largely been carried by Middle Eastern governments. The study indicated that applications for funding may be more successful when planning long-term storage requirements if they include an accurate and detailed budget (Appendix 1). Long-term planning, however, requires estimations of spaces for processing, storage, study and conservation. The formula shown here has been created for calculating the floor space required for the project life to assist in estimating future space requirements based on study findings:

Building floor capacity (m^2) =
a = years of project
b = study years (no artefacts collected)
x = crates per annum*
y = optimisation factor (x 16)*
*Full crate size (L 52cm x W 35cm x H 30cm) optimised @ 16 per m^2

Example:
a = projected project life of 20 years
b = 4 study years
x = average accumulation rate of 78 crates per annum
y = 16 crates per m²
Projected floor space requirements = $78x \frac{(20-4)}{16} = 78m^2$

It may be adapted for specific project timelines such as five, ten, fifteen or twenty year periods. Its scope does not include outdoor acreage requirements for quantities of large architectural objects. This example is based on a project which plans to operate for twenty years. Four years have been scheduled for study seasons where no excavation will take place. By using the average crate accumulation rate (78) divided by the years of operation (20) then divided by the optimised crate factor (16) the formula provides a projected floor space storage requirement of 78m² for this term.

Funding

The study found the requirement of long-term care for archaeological collections is not being met by the supply of adequate funding. Survey participants indicated that obtaining adequate funding was always problematic, even though 88% of them receive government funding. Government funding is that provided by a commonwealth entity that advises governments on research matters, whereas 64% of participants specified they received private funding. Private funding may be provided by a particular company or individual deciding to fund a project. However, 53% of participants specified that they received funding from university departments that are divisions of a university or school faculty devoted to the discipline of archaeology or anthropology. Only 29% of participants specified that funding was on-going, and similarly another 29% said they received grants for three to five years, while 25% specified that they received grants for one to three years. A further 23% of participants reported that they received funding from private institutions that study archaeological themes and are controlled by a private individual(s). 14% of participants received funding from university institutions which are incorporated units within a university and often attached to a museum. A further 14% recorded that they received commercial funding and 13% of participants said their funding was comprised of a 'mosaic' of grants (Appendix 2). The study found that applying for funds is time-consuming and competitive and that capital expenditure for building and maintenance costs are not usually granted. This is an area of major concern for archaeologists, conservators and curators. To overcome funding shortfalls, additional sources of income, such as that derived from field schools and volunteer programs, operated at two case study sites.

Directorates and Museums

The archaeological process involves interactions with directorate personnel at archaeological sites and in regional and/or national museums. However, formal agreements which set out terms for access to and use of accessioned artefacts or collections for scientific or educational use are generally not entered into between archaeologists and hosting country directorates. As a result this can lead to misunderstandings and uncertainty on behalf of both parties. 70% of surveyed archaeologists indicated that artefacts and collections were easily accessible and 64% indicated that artefacts were in good condition when examined. 56% indicated that artefacts and collections had an accompanying archive and 50% reported that museum staff had a good knowledge of artefacts and collections (Appendix 2).

Local directorates are responsible for reviewing and evaluating pre-existing collections and the museums that manage them. Archaeological project directors are responsible for reviewing and evaluating pre-existing collections stored at archaeological sites, which includes registration, cataloguing and classification. Archaeologists are responsible for transporting artefacts to museums. Directorate personnel are responsible for accessioning new artefacts and collections into museums and are responsible for keeping copies of administrative records for accessioned artefacts and/or collections of artefacts with reference to location, content and reports. Directorates are financially responsible for caring for collections in museums that are funded through centralised ministries for curatorial costs. Directorates charge international archaeologists permit fees for conducting surveys or excavation projects in host countries and these fees contribute towards administrative and curatorial costs. These may include funds for storage, inventory, maintenance, conserving, and publications and for providing access to collections. Some permit fees are significantly reduced for international projects that aim to conduct activities which rehabilitate, manage and conserve archaeological sites rather than excavate. Directorates use state-owned national and regional museums, educational or scientific institutions for curating archaeological collections.

Regional museums play a central role in administering archaeological activities and accession artefacts and collections recovered as a result of survey or excavation from archaeological sites generally in the surrounding region. Some objects may be accessioned into national museums. Formal contracts between directorates and archaeological project directors that specify costs, special procedures, instructions, terms for access and use, records needs, inventories and inspections or discard policies are not generally entered into. Cultural heritage legislation in many Middle Eastern countries contains few guidelines for accessioning artefacts, organising and managing on-site archaeological collections, or for accessing them once deposited. This absence of detail in current regulations has allowed a mediocre standard of archaeological collections management practice to be conducted in countries and states that host archaeological activities.

Accessing Archaeological Collections in Museums, On-Site and Remotely

There are no regulations which specify that a museum will make artefacts or collections available to archaeologists for scientific or educational use, and likewise there are no specifications in current regulations for researchers to access on-site archaeological storage depots. Formal applications must be made in advance through directorate administrative channels for access to museum artefacts. Artefacts stored in on-site depots may be accessed during a study or excavation season after proper application is made. Almost all archaeological artefacts and collections remain in their country of origin unless permission is expressly given for external scientific and destructive testing on samples, or unless they are formally loaned for research or exhibition purposes. But because physical access to artefacts and collections may not always be possible, the availability of digital information about artefacts and collections is therefore necessary for research and other purposes. Two of the case study sites provide access to research data via their websites (Appendix 1). The Çatalhöyük Research Project provides an online database that gives direct access to updated excavation and other specialist data recorded during the season. Databases can be accessed by browsing categories of information or by conducting specific quick or complex searches on units, buildings, spaces, features, or objects.[75] Tell Ta'yinat with the CRANE (Computational Research on the Ancient Near East) project provides a platform for data integration and analysis from the Orontes Watershed of southeast Turkey and northwest Syria. With the University of Chicago the Online Cultural and Historical Research Environment (OCHRE) has been created that records, integrates, analyses, publishes and preserves cultural and historical information in digital forms. A key aspect is to create websites which enable direct access to primary data. Websites are used by team members to record data and a means for the project to reach out to wider, non-archaeological audiences. General information on an archaeological project website includes history and sources of primary data in on-line databases.[76] Receiving a full site archive from archaeological project directors recording comprehensive details

---

[75] Case study No. 3, Çatalhöyük Research Project Research Portal. Website: http://www.catalhoyuk.com/database/catal/Search.asp (18/08/2016); see also case study No. 4, Tell Ta'yinat CRANE Projects Website: https://www.crane.utoronto.ca/tell-tayinat.html (18/08/2016); University of Chicago OCHRE Data Service Website: https://ochre.uchicago.edu/ (18/08/2016).
[76] Forte *et al.* 2015; see also Axiell Group 2016. *Archival, Museum and Library Standards.* Webpage: http://alm.axiell.com/expertise/standards(20/08/2016); Archaeological Archives Forum 2010; Institute for Archaeologists 2008b. *Standard and Guidance for the creation, compilation, transfer and deposition of archaeological archives*; Schlanger 2002; NPS 1997 *Determining museum storage space requirements*; Ganiaris and Starling 1996.

about archaeological collections is not a legal requirement in many Middle Eastern countries. Current reporting requirements do not adequately reflect all of the information that is gleaned through fieldwork and collecting activities.

Implementing Archaeological Collections Management Strategies

Recommendations for Governments

The study found the indirect effects of current legislation and current practice lead to deterioration, damage and destruction of archaeological artefacts and collections, particularly those stored at archaeological sites. The following recommendations are provided for governments that host archaeological missions to implement over the next five years:

Review cultural heritage legislation for managing archaeological collections related to:

    a) Governance
    b) Current management, strategies and approaches
    c) Phases of archaeological process
    d) Written or formal policies
    e) Components of collections
    f) Documentation systems and digital archive
    g) Storage provision and future expansion needs

Evaluate the current archaeological collections management practice related to:

    a) Management planning
    b) Documentation
    c) Resource management
    d) Collections assessment
    e) Collections management
    f) Collections management systems
    g) Conservation and preservation
    h) Access and use of collections
    i) Collections significance criteria
    j) Security

Incorporate specific requirements in legislation for managing archaeological collections related to:

    a) Cataloguing
    b) Classification and conservation systems
    c) Handling and packing
    d) Inventory and security
    e) Object cleaning and conservation
    f) Object identification

    g) Pest management and housekeeping
    h) Quantifying collections
    i) Registering artefacts
    j) Writing an archaeological collections management plan
    k) Accessioning

Recommendations for Funding Bodies

The majority of archaeological research is funded by governmental bodies which are theoretically committed to the highest standards of integrity in all aspects of research that they support.[77] This includes ensuring that research is conducted according to appropriate ethical, legal and professional frameworks, obligations and standards. Standards for preserving archaeological collections involve implementing preventive measures and controlling environmental conditions. The study showed these are the most critical elements for ensuring long-term protection of archaeological collections. A key threat has been identified as the lack of understanding and financial support of these requirements by funding bodies. In accordance with institutional policy requirements for managing storage of research data and primary materials responsibly, recommendations for granting indirect cost budget items that are necessary for long-term preservation of archaeological collections include:

    a) Capital works and general infrastructure for construction of storage depots adequate for the life of an archaeological project and beyond.
    b) General maintenance of storage depots.

Recommendations for Archaeologists

The circumstances of a project dictate the development and extent of documentation systems. These will depend on the size of a project and the type and range of activities. Any system will also depend on the processes and interactions, and the competence of personnel. For an archaeological project to function effectively it has to identify and manage numerous linked activities. Although there are no legal requirements or standards for how archaeological projects should do this in the Middle East, international standards for good practice require that management systems be documented. Even though an archaeological project has flexibility in what, or if, it chooses to document its systems, it should develop the amount of documentation it needs to demonstrate effective planning, operation, control and continual improvement of its management system and processes. Written policies and procedure for these archaeological collections management processes are recommended as a minimum on-site standard:

---

[77] The Australian Code for the Responsible Conduct of Research 2007, Section 2.6 Manage storage of research data and primary materials.

a) Recording
b) Collecting and sampling
c) Registration and packing
d) Cleaning and washing
e) Sorting and classification
f) Cataloguing
g) Inventory
h) Labelling
i) Conservation
j) Photography and illustration
k) Analysis
l) Materials analysis
m) Classification
n) Data entry
o) Storage
p) Accessing

Summary

Reasons for Managing Archaeological Collections

Current archaeological practice across a wide demographic and geographic range of archaeologists, conservators and curators was examined and found wanting. Analysing data from the literature review, survey and field study allowed new data-sets to be created referencing how archaeological collections are currently managed. It indicates that more needs to be known about how collections contained in on-site storage depots are managed. A need was highlighted for a practical method that would address existing backlogging and that would also have assessment criteria for old, perhaps redundant, objects to help clear storage depots and to help justify decisions to discard. Criteria were also needed to manage artefacts coming in from the field each season. In the short-term process, artefacts were stored in conditions relative to their importance, compared to less important ones, but in the long-term artefacts were stored in conditions relative to their physical characteristics and stability. The research indicated that plans must contain policies that are clear, concise and understood by all persons working on-site due to the turnover in personnel. Multi-lingual guidelines must state what is being done, why it is happening and the way it is to be done. The intent of the project should be accurately recorded in a documentary system which produces files, records and a full project archive. The plan must suit a range of compatible IT and data manipulation systems. A compatible system that could be used both by local governments (and museums) and archaeological project directors (and institutes) is needed. By adopting the recommended quality-based measures project directors would better demonstrate their commitment to delivering stakeholder benefits and would improve the cost-effectiveness of their archaeological projects. They would extend the impact of their collections-based activities and enhance their credibility with funders, partners and supporters. Actions like these enable more confidence, flexibility and openness to innovation and provide clarity around roles and responsibilities. Another benefit is that strategic decision-making around expenditure and investment is supported by facts. A quality-based approach should include training initiatives and opportunities for professional development that can be built upon. Project directors should have improved ability through better access to funds for these costs so as to build on change and thus improve.

Code for Managing Archaeological Collections Into the Future

Fundamentally, artefacts are valuable because they are immediately linked with the scientific process and are able to provide data relative to the size and scope of the collections for analyses. Responsible and proper treatment of artefacts

Summary

throughout the archaeological process upholds the integrity of science through good practice and facilitates the progress of scientific activities. Codes of conduct for responsible research verify this. Researchers must manage research data and primary materials in accordance with the policy of their institutions by keeping clear and accurate records of the research methods and data sources. They must ensure that research data and primary materials are kept in safe and secure storage even when not in use. They must provide the same level of care and protection for primary research records as for the analysed research data. They must retain research data, including electronic data, in a durable, indexed and retrievable form. They must maintain a catalogue of research data in an accessible form and manage it and the primary materials according to ethical protocols and relevant legislation. But even so, for artefacts or collections to be of scientific value, rather than an ever-increasing drain on a project's resources, the artefacts themselves must also justify the resources they use. This is an important aspect for project directors to justify. It can be done by developing and implementing detailed plans to explain their archaeological collections management activities in more detail. For these and many more reasons, the long-term preservation and maintenance of artefacts must be featured more highly in project planning. This means systematic documentation of all of the processes involved in managing artefacts and collections. This includes, but is not limited to: recording, in-field collecting, conservation and sampling; processing, washing, sorting and classification; registration; cataloguing; labelling and packing; post-excavation conservation; storage and curation; inventory control; data management; discard; and access and use. This plan was designed for use by archaeological project directors wishing to adopt and implement more strategic and integrated approaches to managing their archaeological collections. It is an approach that observes sustainable principles to consolidate archaeological processes and which was formulated based on the needs identified by the study. It accounts for the legal and ethical requirements to which parties are subject. Its purpose is to provide a common definition of professional practice for local governments and archaeologists working in the Middle East. It can be used in full, in part, or as a basic checklist to help implement 'quality' site-specific collections management practices that are most adaptable, practical and sustainable. Figure 12 shows the basic elements of an archaeological collections management plan.

Scope	General
	Application
	Goals
	Terms and definitions
Management system	General requirements
	Management structure
	Management responsibilities
	Regulatory responsibilities
	Management planning and system review
Documentation	General
	Operational procedures
	Control of documents
	Control of records
Resource management	Provision of resources
	Human resources
	Infrastructure
Collections assessment	Estimation of collections
	Collections scope and size
	Significance criteria
Collections management	Objectives
	Policies and procedures
	Records and data management
	Access and use
Inventory management	Annual inventory
	Object locations
	Annual report
Security	Succession plan
	Emergency planning/disaster response
	Threats to archaeological collections
	Threats to documentary archive

FIGURE 12: ELEMENTS OF AN ARCHAEOLOGICAL COLLECTIONS MANAGEMENT PLAN.

Glossary

ACMP	A template to assist in developing orderly and sustainable procedures for the long-term management and curation of Near Eastern archaeological artefact collections excavated from research and salvage sites.
ARCHAEOLOGICAL ARTEFACTS AND COLLECTIONS	a) The material collection which consists of all objects (artefacts, building materials or environmental remains) and associated samples of contextual materials or objects. b) The documentary collection which consists of all records made during an archaeological project, including those in hard copy and digital form.
ARCHAEOLOGICAL ARCHIVE: RECORDS AND FILES	Consists of paper and digital records integral to the site, which include photographs, negatives, field notes, excavation profiles, artefact catalogues, GIS and field reports, digital media and correspondence generated by the project and which correspond with all three-dimensional object collections.
CLASSIFICATION	The systematic arrangement of objects or collections based on characteristics, such as type, form, origin or function.
CONSERVATOR	Qualified professional who specialises in the stabilising treatment of archaeological artefacts.
CONTROLLED VOCABULARY	The facility to restrict and monitor the terms or words which may be recorded in a specific field.
DATA	Information stored on a computer or manual system.
DATABASE	A system allowing the recording, organisation and retrieval of data.
FRAMEWORK	A management system which establishes, documents and implements continual improvement and effectiveness.

INVENTORY	Documented count of all artefacts and collections of artefacts stored on-site conducted annually. A list of all artefacts and collections and their locations. The content and location of the project archive.
MANAGEMENT	The scholar(s) or individual(s) who are responsible to the local ministry for the scientific, financial and administrative affairs of the on-going excavation, survey or sondage.
MUSEUM	A museum under the responsibility of a centralised antiquities directorate.
POLICY	A document setting out a course of action.
PROCEDURE	A series of actions conducted in a certain order or manner.
PROCESS	A series of actions or proceedings used in achieving something.
PROJECT DIRECTOR (PROJECT MANAGEMENT)	The scholar or individual who is the permit holder and who is responsible to the local ministry for the scientific, financial and administrative affairs of the on-going excavation, survey or sondage.
REGISTER; CATALOGUE	A paper record of all objects which are or have been part of the project's archaeological collections.

Bibliography

Ad hoc Group for Inventory and Documentation. 2009. *Guidance on inventory and documentation of the cultural heritage*. Strasbourg: Council of Europe.

Albright, W. 1923. The Annual of the American Schools of Oriental Research, Vol. 4, Excavations and Results at Tell el-Fûl (Gibeah of Saul) (1922–1923), pp. iii–160. *The American Schools of Oriental Research.*

Alexandri, A. 2002. Names and emblems: Greek archaeology, regional identities and national narratives at the turn of the 20th century. *Antiquity* 76, p. 291.

American Association of Museums. 2004. *The AAM Guide to Collections Planning.* Washington: AAM. 2003. *Information Center Fact Sheet: Outline for a Collections Plan.* Washington: AAM.

1984. *Caring for Collections: Strategies for Conservation, Maintenance, and Documentation.* Washington, DC: American Association of Museums.

Arab Republic of Egypt. 2011. Supreme Council of Antiquities. Arab Republic of Egypt, Supreme Council of Antiquities, 2011. *http://www.sca-egypt.org/eng/sca_history.htm* (19/11/2013).

2010. *Ministry of Culture Law* No. 117 of 1983 as amended by Law No. 3 of 2010. 1983. *Law on the Protection of Antiquities.* 1951. *Law No. 215 on the Protection of Antiquities.* 1912. *Ministerial Order No. 51 for the Export of Antiquities.*

1912. *Ministerial Order No. 52. Regulations for Excavations.*

1912. *Law No. 14 on the Antiquities of Egypt.*

Archaeological Archives Forum. 2010. *Developing an Archaeological Resource Centre: Guidance for Sustainable Storage and Access to Museum Collections.* University of Reading: IfA.

Archaeological Institute of America. 2008. *Code of Professional Standards.*

Aslan, Z. 2014. Education and Professionalisation for Heritage Conservation in the Arab Region: Review of Current Status and Strategic Directions. *Conservation and Management of Archaeological Sites*, 16, pp. 117–130.

Australia – ICOMOS Inc. 2014. *The Burra Charter.*

2013. *The Burra Charter and Archaeological Practice.* Website: http://australia.icomos.org/wp-content/uploads/Practice-Note_The-Burra-Charter-and-Archaeological-Practice.pdf (12/08/2015).

2004. *The Illustrated Burra Charter.*

1999. *Burra Charter (Revised) for the Conservation of Places of Cultural Significance.*

Website: http://australia.icomos.org/publications/charters/ (12/08/2015).

Australian Association of Consulting Archaeologists Inc. 2012. *Code of Ethics.* Australian Government. 2014. *Australian Best Practice Guide to Collecting Cultural Material.* Canberra: Ministry for the Arts. 2014.

Guidelines for Expert Examiners under the Protection of Movable Cultural Heritage Act 2007. *Australian Code for the Responsible Conduct of Research.*

Axiell Group. 2016. *Archival, Museum and Library Standards.* Website: http://alm.axiell.com/expertise/standards (20/08/2016).

Baca, M., Harpring, P., Lanzi, E., McRae, L., and Whiteside, A. 2006. *Cataloging Cultural Objects: A Guide to Describing Cultural Works and Their Images.* Chicago: American Library Association.

Banning, E. 2000. *The Archaeologist's Laboratory. The Analysis of Archaeological Data.* Toronto: Springer.

Boast, R. 2002. Mortimer Wheeler's science of order: the tradition of accuracy at Arikamedu. *Antiquity* 76, p. 291.

2009. The Formative Century, 1860-1960. In Cunliffe, B., Gosden, C., and Joyce, R. (eds.), *The Oxford Handbook of Archaeology.* Oxford: Oxford University Press, pp. 47–70.

Bowdler, S. 1981. Unconsidered Trifles? Cultural Resource Management, Environmental Impact Statements and Archaeological Research in New South Wales. *Australian Archaeology*, 12, pp. 123–133.

Braunholtz, H. 1953. History of Ethnography in the Museum. *The British Museum Quarterly,* 18, pp. 109–120.

British Standards Institution. 2009. *PAS 197:2009. Code of Practice for Collections Management.*

Brown, D. 2011. *Safeguarding Archaeological Information – Procedures for minimising risk to undeposited archaeological archives.* English Heritage.

Bryn Mawr College. 2006. *Collections Management Policy.*

Bryson, J. 2016. *Managing Information Services: An Innovative Approach*, 4th Edition. Routledge.

Buck, R. and Gilmore, J. (eds.) 1998. *The New Museum Registration Methods.* Washington DC: American Association of Museums.

California State Parks. 2009. *Guidelines for Writing a Scope of Collections Statement.* Archaeology, History & Museums Division, Museum Services Section.

Cassidy, J. and Guerre L. 2009. *Finds Guidance.* The Çatalhöyük Research Project.

Çatalhöyük Research Project. 2016. *Research Portal.* Website: http://www.catalhoyuk.com/database/catal/Search.asp (18/08/2016).

2009. *Notes for Excavators.* The Çatalhöyük Research Project.

2009. *The Location Register.* The Çatalhöyük Research Project.

2009. *'X' Finds*. The Çatalhöyük Research Project.

2004. Çatalhöyük *Management Plan*. Euromed: The TEMPER Project.

Childs, S. 2010. Managing Archaeological Collections in the United States: how do we make the process sustainable? Paper presented at the symposium *Developing Sustainable, Strategic Collection Management Approaches for Archaeological Collections*, Melbourne Museum (11–12 November).

Clark, G. 1982. Quantifying Archaeological Research. *Advances in Archaeological Method and Theory*, 5, pp. 217–273.

Commission of the European Communities. 2013. *Mediterranean Cultural Heritage, A Manual for Good Practice*. Oxfordshire: Libri Publishing.

Committee for Documentation of Cultural Heritage. 2011. CIPA Heritage Documentation. *Best Practices in the Management of Archaeological World Heritage Sites.*

Council of Europe. 1992. European Convention for the Protection of the Archaeological Heritage of Europe (Revised).

Davis, H. 1972. The Crisis in American Archeology. *Science*, 175, pp. 267–272.

De Beer, G. 1953. Sir Hans Sloane and the British Museum. *The British Museum Quarterly*, 18, pp. 2–4.

Deeben, J., Goenewoudt, B., Hellewas, D., and Willems, W. 1999. Proposals for a Practical System of Significance Evaluation in Archaeological Heritage Management. *European Journal of Archaeology* 2, pp. 177–199.

Demas, M. 2003. *The GCI Project Bibliographies Series – Conservation and Management of Archaeological Sites.* Los Angeles: The Getty Conservation Institute, pp. 13–68.

Directorate of Antiquities Jordan. 2015. *Regulations for Archaeological Projects in Jordan based on the provisions of the Jordanian Antiquities Law No. 21 for the year 1988 and its amendments.*

Directorate of Culture and Cultural and Natural Heritage Regional Co-operation Division. 2011. *Guidance on the Development of Legislation and Administration Systems in the Field of Cultural Heritage.* Strasbourg: Council of Europe.

2008. *Analysis and reform of cultural heritage policies in South-East Europe*. Strasbourg: Council of Europe.

Dollery, D. 1994. A Methodology of Preventive Conservation for a Large, Expanding and Mixed Archaeological Collection. *Studies in Conservation* 39, pp. 69–72.

Doumas, C. 2013. Managing the Archaeological Heritage: The Case of Akrotiri, Thera (Santorini). *Conservation and Management of Archaeological Sites,* 15, pp. 109–120.

EDINA. 2014. *MANTRA Research Data Management Training.* http://datalib.edina.ac.uk/mantra/(29/08/2015).

Eidem, J. 1998. The 'Tishrin Project' and Salvage Archaeology – *The Tishrin Dam Area. Proceedings of the International Symposium held at Barcelona, January 28th–30th 1998*, Barcelona, Aula Orientalis – Supplementa 15, 1999, pp. 19–24.

English Heritage. 2012. *The UK Historic Environment Data Standard.* Midas Heritage.

2008. Conservation Principles: Policies and Guidance for the Sustainable Management of the Historic Environment.

Ertürk, N. 2011. A management model for archaeological site museums in Turkey. *Museum Management and Curatorship,* 21, pp. 336–348.

Fagan, B. 1995. Archaeology's Dirty Secret. *Archaeology,* 48, pp. 14–17.

Fisher, C. 1925. A Plan for the Systematic Coordination of Archaeological Research in Palestine and Syria. *Bulletin of the American Schools of Oriental Research, 18.*

Fitzpatrick, D. 2015. *Collections at Risk: An examination of archaeological collections management practices in the Near East.* PhD diss., University of Melbourne.

Forte, M., DellÚnto, N., and Haddow, S. 2015. Cyber Archaeology. How 3D Modelling is unpeeling the Neolithic at Çatalhöyük. *World Archaeology,* 61, pp. 36–40.

Ganiaris, H. and Starling, K. 1996. Up to standard: planning the needs of an archaeological archive. *Studies in Conservation,* 41, pp. 55–58.

Getty Conservation Institute. 2003. The GCI Project Bibliographies Series. Conservation and Management of Archaeological Sites.

Golfomitsou, S. and Rico, T. 2014. Perspectives from the Arabian Peninsula. *Conservation and Management of Archaeological Sites,* 16, pp. 99–104.

Greene, J. 1999. Preserving which past for whose future? The dilemma of cultural resource management in case studies from Tunisia, Cyprus and Jordan. *Conservation and Management of Archaeological Sites,* 3, pp. 43–60.

Grey, T. 2006. *Archaeological Finds Procedures Manual.* Museum of London Archaeology Service.

Griset, S. and M. Kodack. 1999. *Guidelines for the Field Collection of Archaeological Materials and Standard Operating Procedures for Curating Department of Defense Archaeological Collections.* St. Louis, MO: Mandatory Center of Expertise for the Curation and Management of Archaeological Collections, U.S. Army Corps of Engineers.

Hall, M. (ed.). 2011. *Towards World Heritage. International Origins of the Preservation Movement 1870–1930.* Farnham: Ashgate Publishing Ltd.

Hashemite Kingdom of Jordan. 2015. *Regulations for Archaeological Projects in Jordan.* Based on the provisions of the Jordanian Antiquities Law No. 21 for the year 1988 as amended 1st January, 2016.

2015. *Draft Regulations for Archaeological Projects in Jordan.* Issued pursuant to the provisions of the Jordanian Antiquities Law No. 21, 1988. Department of Antiquities of Jordan.

2014. Department of Antiquities of Jordan. *The Strategy for Management of Jordan's Archaeological Heritage 2014-2018.* USAID.

2005. *Law No. 5 of 2005 on the Protection of Immovable Heritage.*

2004. *Antiquities Law No. 21, 1988 and modified Law No. 23, 2004.*

1993. *Decision on the Site of Petra.*

1991. Regulations of Archaeological Excavations in accordance with the provisions of the Law of Antiquities No. 21 of 1988.

1988. *Law No.14 (modified) of 1988 on Antiquities.*

1988. *Regulations for Archaeological Projects in Jordan.* Antiquities Law No. 21 for the year 1988 with its amendments.

1976. *Temporary Law No.12 of 1976 on Antiquities.*

1975. *Rules of Excavation.*

1966. *Law on Archaeological Sites.*

1953. *Antiquities Order No.1 made in virtue of Article 34 of the Antiquities Law.*

1923. *Antiquities Ordinance of Palestine.*

Heritage Collections Council. 1998. reCollections: Caring for Collections Across Australia. Managing Collections. http://www.amol.org.au/ (22/11/12).

Heritage Council of Victoria. 2014. Assessing the cultural heritage significance of places and objects for possible state heritage listing: The Victorian Heritage Register Criteria and Threshold Guidelines.

Heritage Victoria. 2014. *Guidelines for Investigating Historical Archaeological Artefacts and Sites.* State Government of Victoria, Department of Transport, Planning and Local Infrastructure.

Historic Scotland. 2006. Guidelines for Project Directors: Dealing with Finds from Projects Sponsored by Historic Scotland.

Institute for Archaeologists. 2008a. *Standard and Guidance for the collection, documentation, conservation and research of archaeological materials.* IfA.

2008b. *Standard and Guidance for the creation, compilation, transfer and deposition of archaeological archives.* IfA.

International Centre for the Study of the Preservation and Restoration of Cultural Property (ICCROM). 2016. *RE-ORG. Tools for Storage Reorganisation and Documentation System.* Website: http://www.unesco.org/new/en/culture/themes/museums/unescoiccrom-re-org/unesco-iccrom-partnership-for-the-preventive-conservation-of-endangered-museum-collections-in-developing-countries-2007-2010/ (15/08/2016).

2011. *International Survey on Museum Storage (summary).* http://bit.ly/19PHY9k (14/08/2015).

2010. *UNESCO-ICCROM Partnership for the Preventive Conservation of Endangered Museum Collections in Developing Countries* (2007–2010). Website: http://www.unesco.org/new/en/culture/themes/museums/unescoiccrom-re-org/unesco-iccrom-partnership-for-the-preventive-conservation-of-endangered-museum-collections-in-developing-countries-2007-2010/ (15/08/2016).

2009. *Brief History.* Website: http://www.iccrom.org/eng/00about_en/00_03history_en.shtml (05/03/2014).

1995. *Conservation on archaeological excavations.* ICCROM.

n.d. *Preventive Conservation for Collections in Storage. Bibliography on Storage Reorganisation.* ICCROM-UNESCO Partnership for the Preventive Conservation of Endangered Museum Collections in Developing Countries.

International Committee for Documentation of Cultural Heritage (CIDOC). 2015. *International Committee for Documentation.* Website: http://icom.museum/the-committees/international-committees/international-committee/international-committee-for-documentation/ (01/08/2015).

1995. CIDOC Fact Sheet No. 1. Registration Step by Step: When an Object Enters the Museum.

1995. International Guidelines for Museum Object Information: the CIDOC Information Categories.

1993. *CIDOC Fact Sheet No. 2. Labelling and Marking Objects.*

1992. Draft International Core Data Standard for Archaeological Sites and Monuments.

International Council of Museums (ICOM). 2012. *ICOM Standards and Guidelines.* http://icom.museum/professional-standards/standards-guidelines/ (06/03/2014).

2012. *Organisation.* Website: http://icom.museum/the-organisation/icom-missions/(16/12/13).

2004. *Running a Museum: A Practical Handbook.*

1995. *Recommendations for the Application of Accession Numbers.*

1995. *International ore Data Standard for Archaeological Sites and Monuments*. 1994. *The NARA document on authenticity.*

1993. *Guidelines for Disaster Preparedness in Museums.*

1986. *Code of Ethics for Museums*. Website: http://www.iccrom.org/eng/00about_en.shtml (16/12/13).

International Council on Monuments and Sites (ICOMOS). 2014 ICOMOS 2014. *Managing Cultural World Heritage*. Website: http://openarchive.icomos.org/1465/ (07/03/2014).

2011. *International Council on Monuments and Sites*. Website: http://www.icomos.org/en/about-icomos/mission-and-vision/statutes-and-policies (16/12/13).

2011a. The Valletta Principles for the Safeguarding and Management of Historic Cities, Towns and Urban Areas.

2011b. *National Committees*. Website: http://www.icomos.org/en/network/national-committees/list-of-national-committees (06/03/2014).

2011c. *Statutes and Policies*. Website: http://www.icomos.org/en/about-icomos/mission-and-vision/statutes-and-policies (16/12/13).

2011d. *CIPA Heritage Documentation. Best Practices and Applications*. Series 1, 2007 and 2009. The ICOMOS & ISPRS Committee for Documentation of Cultural Heritage.

2010. *Management plans and the World Heritage Convention: A bibliography.*

2005. *Xi'an Declaration on the Conservation of the Setting of Heritage Structures, Sites and Areas.*

2002. Management and Preservation of Archaeological Sites. *4th Bilaterial Meeting of ICOMOS Turkey – ICOMOS GREECE 29 April–2 May 2002, SIDE* (Antalya-Turkey).

1999a. *Operational Guidelines for the implementation of World Heritage Convention (Revised).*

1999b. *International Cultural Tourism Charter – Managing Tourism at Places of Heritage Significance.*

1999c. *Principles for the Preservation of Historic Timber Structures.*

1999d. *Charter on the Built Vernacular Heritage.*

1964. *Venice Charter for the Conservation and Restoration of Monuments and Sites.*

International Committee on Archaeological Heritage Management. 2010. *International Cultural Tourism Charter* (01/08/2015).

2010. Draft Guidelines for the Charter for the Protection and Management of the Archaeological Heritage.

2009. *Charters.* Website: http://www.icomos.org/icahm/index.html (14/03/2014).

2008. Eger-Xi'an Principles. Objectives and Procedures of the International Committee on Archaeological Heritage Management.

1990. *Charter for the Protection and Management of the Archaeological Heritage.* International Committee for the Management of Archaeological Heritage (ICAHM).

International Institute of Intellectual Co-Operation. 1940. *Manual on the Technique of Archaeological Excavations.* International Museums Office.

International Scientific Committee on Archaeological Heritage Management (ICAHM). 2010. Draft Guidelines for the Charter for the Protection and Management of the Archaeological Heritage.

2010. *International Cultural Tourism Charter* (01/08/2015).

2009. *ICAHM.* Website: http://www.icomos.org/icahm/index.html (14/03/2014

2008. *Draft Guidelines for the Charter for the Protection and Management of the Archaeological Heritage.* http://ip51.icomos.org/icahm/importantdocs.html (01/08/2015).

International Organisation for Standardisation (ISO). 2000. International ISO Standard 9001:2000 (E). *Quality Management Systems – Requirements.*

Iraq Museum. 2013. *The Iraq Museum.* http://www.theiraqmuseum.com/pages/about-the-museum/(02/12/2013).

Israel Antiquities Authority. 2011. http://www.antiquities.org.il/Article_list_eng.asp?sub_menu=2&section_id=38&Module_id=11 (27/11/2013).

Kaeser, M. 2002. On the international roots of prehistory. *Antiquity,* 76, pp. 170–177.

Kantner, J. 2008. The Archaeology of Regions: From Discrete Analytical Toolkit to Ubiquitous Spatial Perspective. *Journal of Archaeological Research*, 16, pp. 37–81.

Kariya, H. and Nielsen, A. 2002. Conservation of Stone Artifacts on Archaeological Sites. *Field Notes: Practical Guides for Archaeological Conservation and Site Preservation No. 13.* Japanese Institute of Anatolian Archaeology.

Kerber, J. 1994. *Cultural Resource Management. Archaeological Research, Preservation Planning, and Public Education in the Northeastern United States.* London: Bergin and Garvey.

Kirk, G. 1946. Archaeological Activities in Palestine and Transjordan since 1939. *Palestine Exploration Quarterly* 72.

Lambert, S. and Mottus, T. 2014. Museum storage space estimations: In theory and practice. In *ICOM-CC 17th Triennial Conference Preprints, Melbourne, 15–19 September 2014,* ed. J. Bridgland, art. 1503, 9 pp. Paris: International Council of Museums.

Lee, E. 2006. *Management of Research Projects in the Historic Environment: The MoRPHE Project Managers' Guide.* http//www.englishheritage.org.uk_publications_morphe-project-planning-note-6_morpheprojectplanningnote6.pdf (30/08/11).

Lynott, M. 1980. Cultural Resource Management. The Dynamics of significance: an example from Central Texas. *American Antiquity*, 45, pp. 117–120.

McIlwaine, J. 2005. *First, Do No Harm. A Register of Standards, Codes of Practice, Guidelines, Recommendation and Similar Works relating to Preservation and Conservation in Libraries and Archives.* International Federation of Library Associations and Institutions (IFLA).

Moratto, M. and Kelly, R. 1978. Optimizing Strategies for Evaluating Archaeological Significance. *Advances in Archaeological Method and Theory.* 1, pp. 1–30.

Murray, T. 2002. Epilogue: why the history of archaeology matters. *Antiquity*, 76, pp. 234–238.

Museum of London Archaeology Service. 1994. *Archaeological Site Manual.* Third Edition.

Museums and Galleries Commission. 2009. *The Small Museums Cataloguing Manual. A guide to cataloguing object and image collections.* Carlton: Museums Australia.

1992. *Standards in the Museum – Care of Archaeological Collections.*

National Archives of Australia. 2002. *Standard for the Physical Storage of Commonwealth Records.*

National Museum of Iceland. 2012. *Guidelines On the Care of Archaeological Artefacts.*

National Park Service (NPS), United States Department of the Interior. 2016. *Glossary Website*: http://www.nps.gov/archeology/collections/glossary.htm (14/07/2016).

2006. *Museum Handbook Part I. Museum Collections.*

2000. *Museum Handbook Part II. Museum Records.*

1998. Museum Handbook Part III. Museum Collections Use.

1997a. Determining museum storage equipment needs. *Conserve O Gram 4/10.* Washington DC. http://1.usa.gov/HPaUTR (14/08/2015).

1997b. Determining museum storage space requirements. *Conserve O Gram 4/11.* Washington DC. http://1.usa.gov/1dbddeM (14/08/2015).

Nordbladh, J. 2002. How to organise oneself within history: Pehr Tham and his relation to antiquity at the end of the 18th century. *Antiquity,* 76, pp. 141–150.

Özen, L. and Spirydowicz, K. 2002. Conservation of Leather & Texile Artifacts on Archaeological Sites. *Field Notes: Practical Guides for Archaeological Conservation and Site Preservation No. 17.* Japanese Institute of Anatolian Archaeology.

Palumbo, G., Al-Tikriti, W., Mahdy, H., Al-Nuaimi, A., Al-Kaabi, A., Altawallbeh, D., Muhammad, S., and Marcus, B. 2014. Protecting the Invisible: Site-Management Planning at Small Archaeological Sites in al-Ain, Abu Dhabi. *Conservation and Management of Archaeological Sites*, 16, pp. 146–62.

Pearce, Susan M. 1996.*Archaeological Curatorship.* Washington, DC: Smithsonian Institution Press.

1992. *Museums, Objects, and Collections.* Washington DC: Smithsonian Institution Press.

1990. *Archaeological Curatorship.* Washington D.C: Smithsonian Institution Press.

Pedeli, C. and Pulga, S. 2013. *Conservation practices on archaeological excavations: principles and methods.* Los Angeles: Getty Institute.

Perrin, K. 2002. *Archaeological Archives: Documentation, Access and Deposition. A Way Forward.* English Heritage.

Poole, N. and A. Dawson. 2013. *SPECTRUM Digital Asset Management V2.0.* Collections Trust.

Poole, N., Dawson, A., and Hillhouse, S. 2015. *Forward Planning for Collections Management. A Good Practice Guide.* London: Collections Trust.

Raab, M. and Klinger, T. 1977. A Critical Appraisal of 'Significance' in Contract Archaeology. *American Antiquity*, 42, pp. 629–634.

Records Management Association of Australasia (RMAA). 2006. *Statement of Knowledge for Recordkeeping Professionals.*

Reibel, D. 2008. *Registration Methods for the Small Museum.* New York: AltaMira Press.

Republic of Turkey. 2012. *Rules & Principles for Conducting Survey, Sondage and Excavations on Cultural and Natural Heritage.* Article 7(1)f.

Republic of the United States of America. 1990. *Curation of Federally Owned and Administered Archaeological Collections Act* (36CFR79).

Richards, J. and Robinson, D. 2000. *Digital Archives from Excavation and Fieldwork: A Guide to Good Practice.* Archaeology Data Service.

Roth, K. and Tsu, M. 2002. Conservation of Unfired Earth Artifacts on Archaeological Sites. *Field Notes: Practical Guides for Archaeological Conservation and Site Preservation No. 14.* Japanese Institute of Anatolian Archaeology.

Russell, R. and K. Winkworth. 2009. *Significance 2.0: a guide to assessing the significance of Collections.* Canberra, Collections Council of Australia Limited.

Schlanger, N. 2002. Ancestral Archives: Explorations in the History of Archaeology. *Antiquity* 76, p. 291.

Schwartz, G.M. 1997. Salvage Excavation. In E.M. Myers (ed.) *The Oxford Encyclopaedia of Archaeology in the Near East*, Vol. 4. New York and Oxford, pp. 459–461.

Sease, C. 1999. *The Role of the Conservator on an Archaeological Excavation.* Japanese Institute of Anatolian Archaeology.

1994. *A Conservation Manual for the Field Archaeologist.* Third Edition. Archaeological Research Tools 4. Los Angeles: Institute of Archaeology, University of California.

Severson, K. and Ersoy, H. 2002. Conservation of Mosaics on Archaeological Sites. *Field Notes: Practical Guides for Archaeological Conservation and Site Preservation No. 18.* Japanese Institute of Anatolian Archaeology.

Singley, K. 1981. Caring for Artifacts After Excavation – Some Advice for Archaeologists. *Historical Archaeology,* 15.

Society of Museum Archaeologists. 1995. *Towards an Accessible Archaeological Archive.*

1993. *Selection, Retention and Dispersal of Archaeological Collections. Guidelines for use in England, Wales and Northern Ireland.* First Edition.

Spirydowicz, K. 2002. Conservation of Wood and Plant Materials on Archaeological Sites. *Field Notes: Practical Guides for Archaeological Conservation and Site Preservation No. 15.* Japanese Institute of Anatolian Archaeology.

Spirydowicz, K. and Özen, L. 2002. Conservation of Bone, Ivory & Antler Artifacts on Archaeological Sites. *Field Notes: Practical Guides for Archaeological Conservation and Site Preservation No. 16.* Japanese Institute of Anatolian Archaeology.

Standards Australia. 2006. *AS ISO/IEC 17025-2005. General requirements for the competence of testing and calibration laboratories.* Sydney: Standards Australia.

2003. *AS ISO 10013-2003 Guidelines for quality management system documentation.* Sydney: Standards Australia.

2002. *AS ISO 15489.1 – 2002 Records Management Part 1: General.* Sydney: Standards Australia.

2002. *AS ISO 15489.2 – 2002 Records Management Part 2: Guidelines.* Sydney: Standards Australia.

Standards Australia International. 2011. *Guide to Standards – Good Management Practice.* SAI.

Standards Australia Limited. 2012. *Standardisation Guide 006: Rules for the Structure and Drafting of Australian Standards.* Sydney: Standards Australia Limited.

Stanley-Price, N. (ed.) 1995. Excavation and Conservation. In, Stanley Price, N. (ed.), *Conservation on Archaeological Excavations.* ICCROM, pp. 1–9.

State Historical Society of North Dakota. 2012. *Guidelines for Submitting Archaeological Collections to the State Historical Society of North Dakota.* North Dakota: SHSND, Archaeology and Historic Preservation Division.

Strahan, D. and Unruh, J. 2002. Conservation of Ceramic Artifacts on Archaeological Sites. *Field Notes: Practical Guides for Archaeological Conservation and Site Preservation No. 12.* Japanese Institute of Anatolian Archaeology.

Sullivan, L. 1992 *Managing Archaeological Resources from the Museum Perspective.* Technical Brief No. 13. Washington, DC: Archaeological Assistance Division, National Park Service, Dept. of the Interior.

Sullivan, S. 1995. A Planning Model for the Management of Archaeological Sites. In Marta de la Torre (ed), *The Conservation of Archaeological Sites in the Mediterranean Region.* Los Angeles: The Getty Conservation Institute, pp. 15–26.

Syrian Arab Republic. 2013. *Syrian Arab Republic, Directorate of Antiquities and Museums.* Webpage: *http://www.dgam.gov.sy/index.php* (27/11/2013).

2010. *A New Vision for Syrian Museums and Cultural Sites*, April 2010.

2010. *A New Vision for the Syrian National Museums and Cultural Heritage Sites – Embargoed Version*, 30 July 2010.

2004. *Act No. 16 on the Accession to the Stockholm Convention for the Protection of Industrial Property.*

2004. *Decree No. 8 on the Accession to the Berne Convention for the Protection of Literary and Artistic Works.*

2001. *Law No. 12 on Copyright.*

2000. *Antiquities Law Legislative Decree #222 of 1963* with Amendments 2000, Chapter 4, Articles 46, 51 and 52.

1999. *Antiquities Law promulgated by Legislative Decree No. 222 of 1963 (Amended).* 1980. *Decree No. 2176.*

1978. *Order No. 170A on Archaeological Monuments.*

1977. *The Decree-law No. 222.* Chapter 4, Article 42.

1968. *Decree No. 1291.*

1963. *Decree-Law No. 222 on the regime of Antiquities in Syria (Antiquities Law).*

Tainter, J. and Lucas, G. 1983. Epistemology of the Significance Concept. *American Antiquity*, 48, pp. 707–719.

Ta'yinat Archaeological Project. 2016. *Tell Ta'yinat.* Website: 2016. http://sites.utoronto.ca/tap/ (05/08/2016).

2016. *CRANE Projects.* Website: https://www.crane.utoronto.ca/tell-tayinat.html (18/08/2016). 2006. *Season Field Manual.* University of Toronto.

Tell Madaba Archaeological Project. 2004. *Excavation Manual.*

Trigger, B. 2007. *A History of Archaeological Thought* (second edition). New York: Cambridge University Press.

1984. Alternative Archaeologies: Nationalist, Colonialist, Imperialist. *Man*, 19, pp. 355–370.

United Nations Educational and Scientific Organisation (UNESCO). 2013. UNESCO Charters and Conventions. http://whc.unesco.org/en/convention/ (07/12/2013).

2008. *Operational guidelines for Implementation of the World Heritage Convention.* World Heritage Centre.

2007. *Documentation of Artefacts' Collections.* Cultural Heritage Protection Handbook 3.

1972a. Convention concerning the Protection of the World Cultural and Natural Heritage.

1972b. Recommendation Concerning the Protection, at National Level, of the Cultural and Natural Heritage.

1956. *Recommendation on International Principles applicable to Archaeological Excavations.* New Delhi.

United States Army Corps of Engineers. 1999. *Guidelines for the Field Collection of Archaeological Materials and Standard Operating Procedures for Curating Department of Defense Archaeological Collections (Final Draft).* St. Louise District: USA Department of Defense.

University of Chicago. 2016. *OCHRE Data Service.* Website: https://ochre.uchicago.edu/ (18/08/2016).

University of Melbourne. 2012. *Procedures and Guidelines for the Management of Research Data and Records.* http://researchdata.unimelb.edu.au/how (29/08/2015).

2005. *Policy on the Management of Research Data and Records.*

Unruh, J. 2012. *On-site interview with Julie Unrhuh,* the Tell Ta'yinat Archaeological Project Conservator (10/07/2012).

2001. A Revised Endpoint for Ceramics Desalination at the Archaeological Site of Gordion, Turkey. *Studies in Conservation,* 46, pp. 81–92.

US National Park Service. 2016. *Glossary.* https://www.nps.gov/archeology/collections/glossary.htm (14/07/2016).

2015. *Glossary.* http://.nps.gov/archeology/collections/glossary.htm (10/09/2015).

Van den Dries, M. and Willems, W. 2007. Quality assurance in Archaeology, the Dutch perspective. In, Willems, W. and Van den Dries, M. (eds.) *Quality Management in Archaeology.* Oxford: Oxbow Books, pp. 50–66.

Waller, R. 2014. *Assessing Risks to Your Collections.* Handbook: A Workshop organised by the National Gallery of Victoria in Melbourne, 8 September, 2014. Protect Heritage Corp.

1994. Conservation risk assessment: a strategy for managing resources for preventive conservation. *Studies in Conservation* 39, pp. 12–16.

Watkins, R., West-Meiers, M., and Visser, Y. 2012. *A Guide to Assessing Needs. Essential Tools for Collecting Information, Making Decisions, and Achieving Development Results.* The World Bank.

Watkinson, D. (ed.) 1981. *First Aid for Finds.* RESCUE – The British Archaeological Trust.

Wharton, G. and Ersoy, H. 2002. Conservation of Metal Artifacts on Archaeological Sites. *Field Notes: Practical Guides for Archaeological Conservation and Site Preservation No. 11.* Japanese Institute of Anatolian Archaeology.

Willems, W. and Brandt, R. 2004. *Dutch Archaeology Quality Standard.*

Willems, W., Kars, H. and Hallewas, D. (eds.) 1997. *Archaeological Heritage Management in the Netherlands. Fifty Years State Service for Archaeological Investigations.* Assen, Van Gorcum.

Willems, W. and Van den Dries, M. (eds.) 2007. *Quality Management in Archaeology.* Oxford: Oxbow Books.

Appendix 1: Field Study: Syria and Turkey

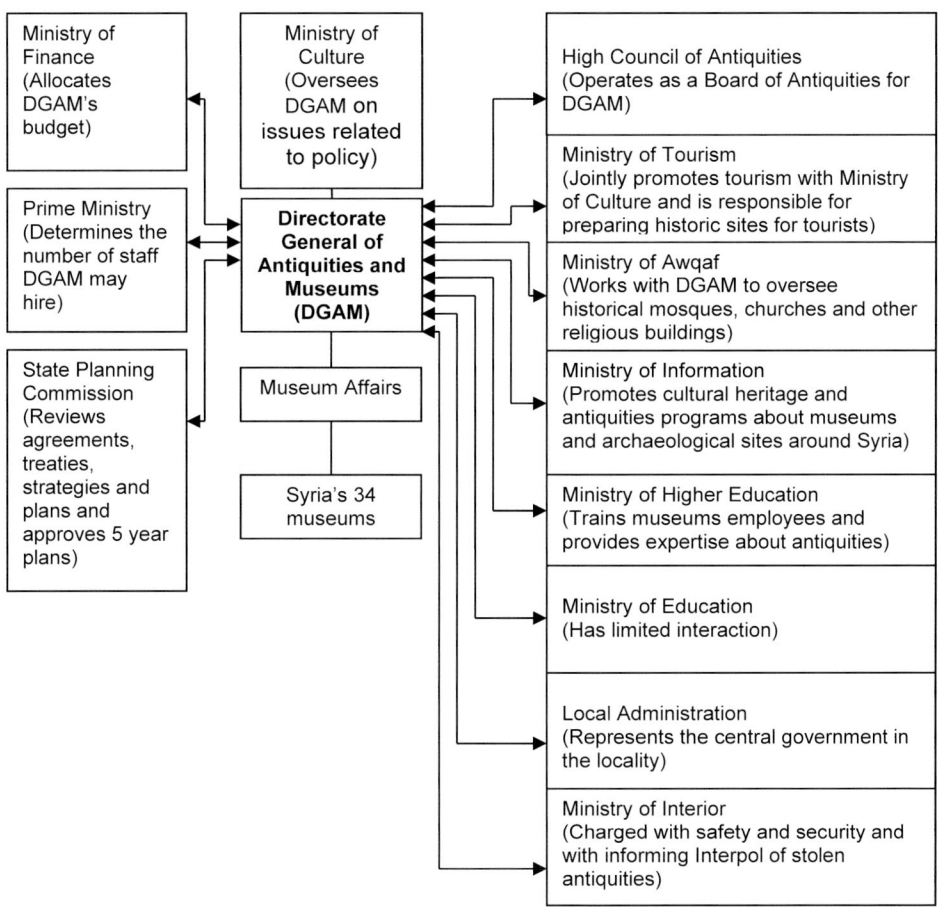

FIGURE 1.1 SYRIAN ARAB REPUBLIC GOVERNANCE STRUCTURE

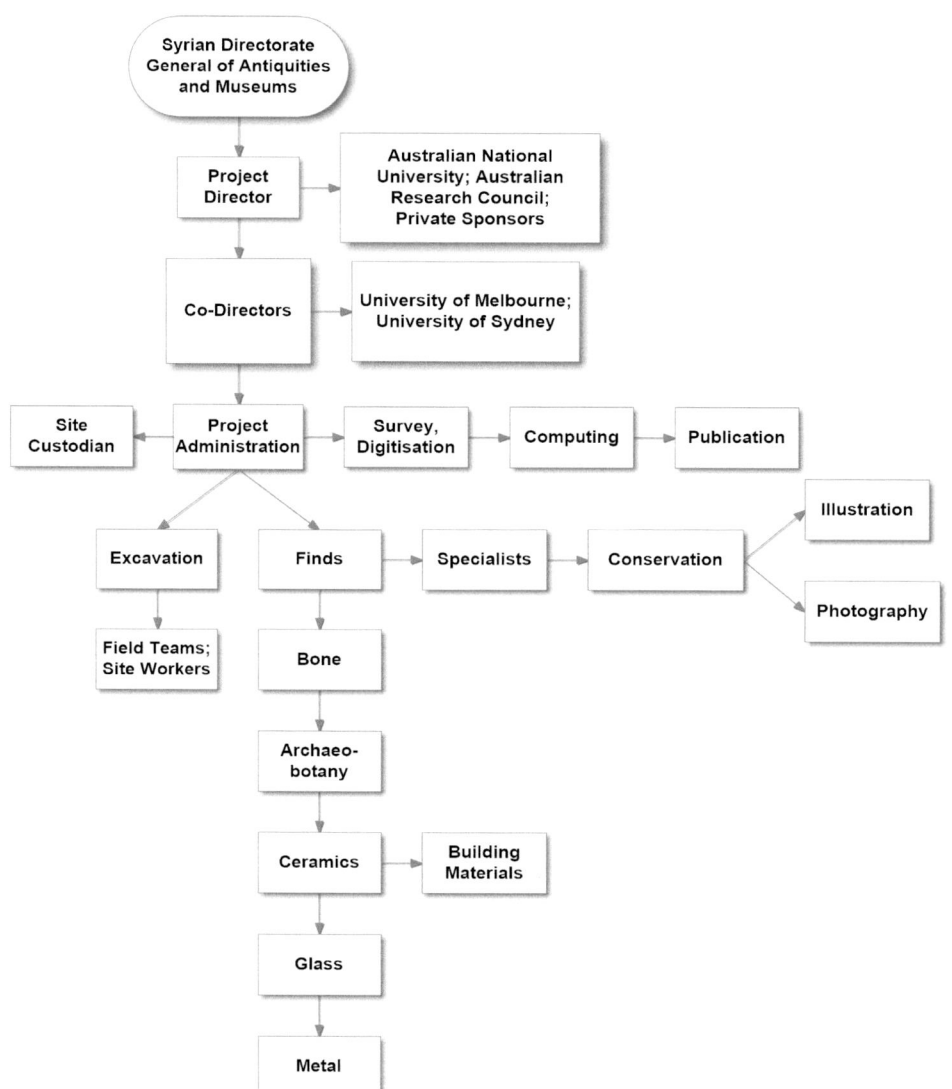

FIGURE 1.2 ORGANISATIONAL STRUCTURE OF JEBEL KHALID IN 2010

Appendix 1: Field Study: Syria and Turkey

Jebel Khalid (April–May 2010)	Area A (Acropolis)	Area S (Domestic quarter)	Area X (Public buildings)	Totals
Excavators	4	7	2	13
Diggers	-	-	-	140
Trenches	3	20	2	25
Trench size	5 m x 10 m	5 m x 5 m	10 m x 10 m	Approx. 850 sqm
Kilograms of body sherds (described, classified, weighed, discarded)	Data not available	757	Data not available	Estimate 1200 kg
Diagnostics (classified, recorded, described not weighed, double-bagged, stored)	Trench 502 (Approx. 200 kg)	Data not available	Data not available	-
Working days		Hours per day	Days	Total hours worked
Excavation		6.0 x 153 persons	22	20,196
Pottery processing		3–6.0 averaged @ 4.5 hrs x 11 persons	19	940.5
Approximation of total cost		AUD $ 100,000		

Figure 1.3 Breakdown of human resources, work hours and quantities excavated

Small Finds Area A Trench 502	
Bone/tooth/antler	4
Ceramic	43
Charcoal	5
Coin	8
Glass	29
Metal	122
Plaster	1
Seed	1
Shell	7
Slag	6
Stone	22
Total	248

Figure 1.4 Inventoried (registered) objects from Area A Trench 502

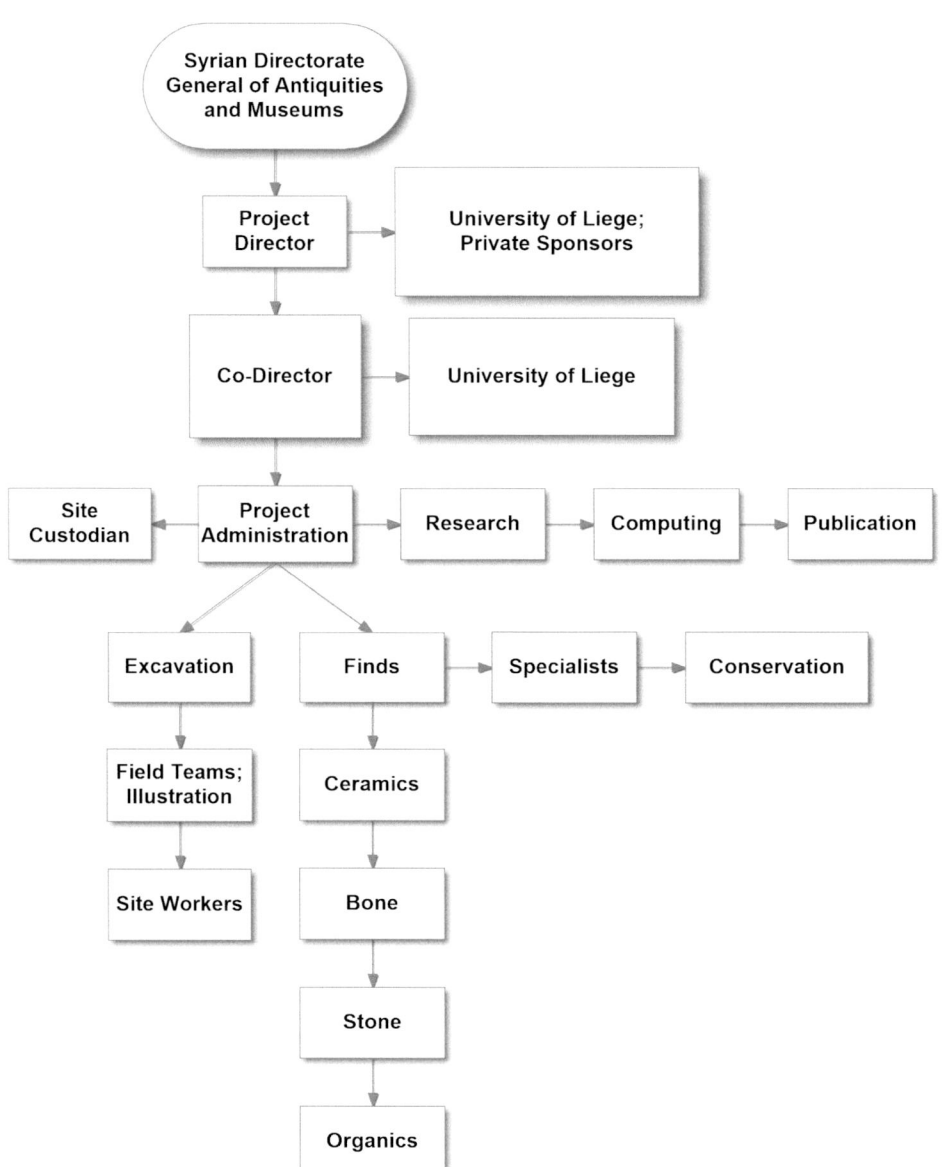

FIGURE 1.5 ORGANISATIONAL STRUCTURE OF TELL AHMAR IN 2010

Tell Ahmar Six-week excavation period (May–June and four-week study period September 2010)	Area M3	Area M14	Area S15	Total
Excavators	2	2	1	5
Diggers				12
Body sherds (washed, bagged stored)	c. 250kg			
Diagnostics (washed, bagged stored)				
Working days		Hours per day	Days	Total Hours worked
Person hours		6.0 x 17 persons	36	3,672
Total cost				Euro 10,000

FIGURE 1.6 BREAKDOWN OF HUMAN RESOURCES, WORK HOURS AND QUANTITIES EXCAVATED IN 2010

Consolidation of Area C Pottery – Tell Ahmar 2010		
Date	People	Total hours
08/06/10	2	18
09/06/10	2	18
10/06/10	2	14
12/06/10	4	36
13/06/10	4	36
15/06/10	4	36
19/06/10	4	36
20/06/10	4	36
Total hours worked		230

FIGURE 1.7 TOTAL HOURS WORKED TO RE-PACK TAH ARCHAEOLOGICAL COLLECTIONS

90 MANAGING ARCHAEOLOGICAL COLLECTIONS IN MIDDLE EASTERN COUNTRIES

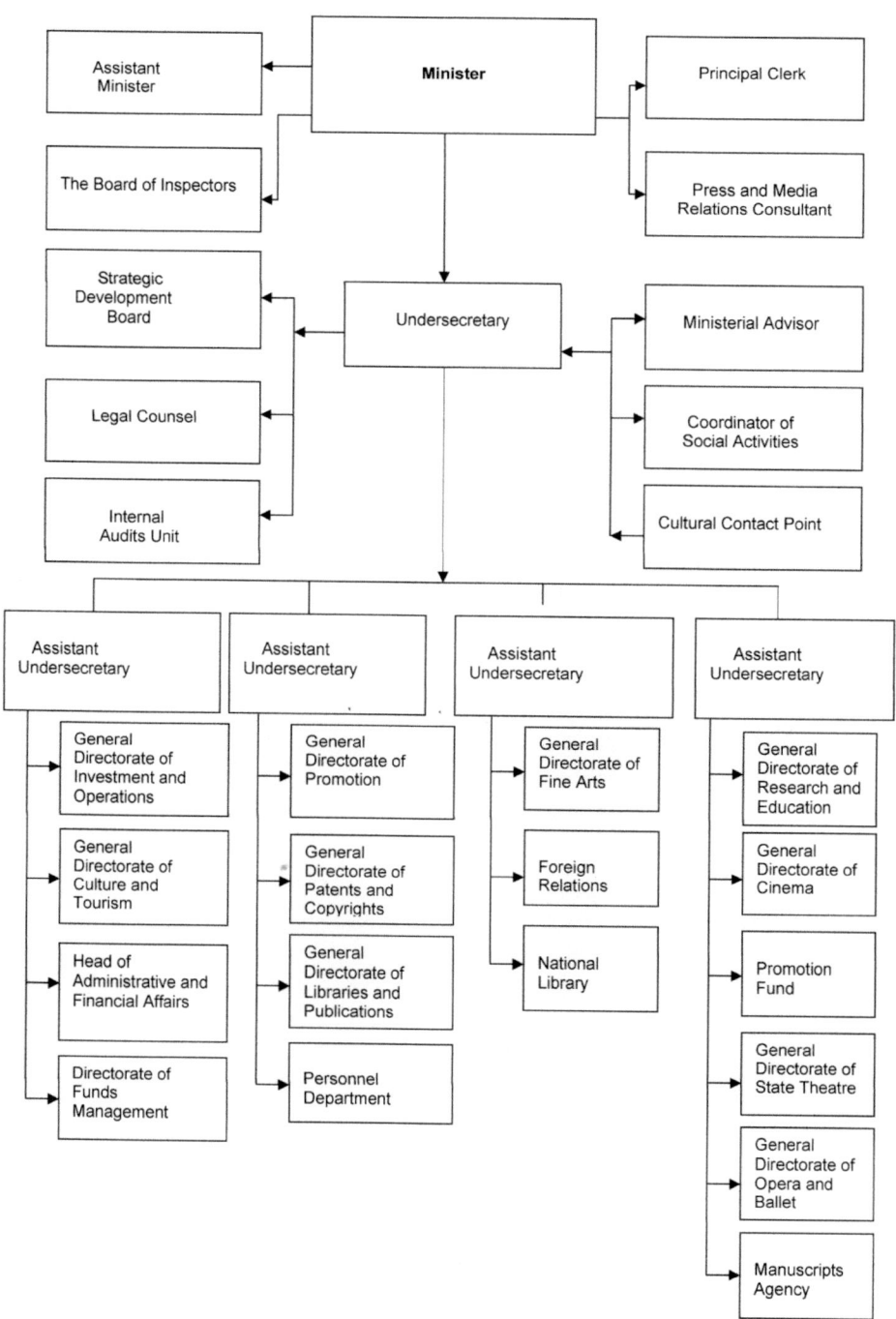

FIGURE 1.8 TURKISH GOVERNMENT CENTRAL ORGANISATION

Appendix 1: Field Study: Syria and Turkey

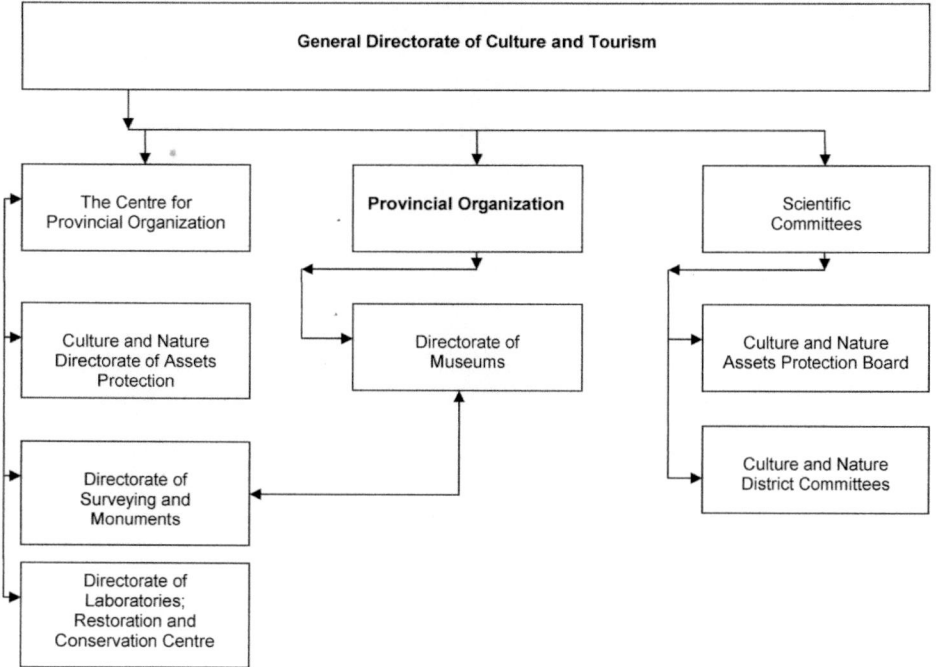

Figure 1.9 Turkish government provincial organization

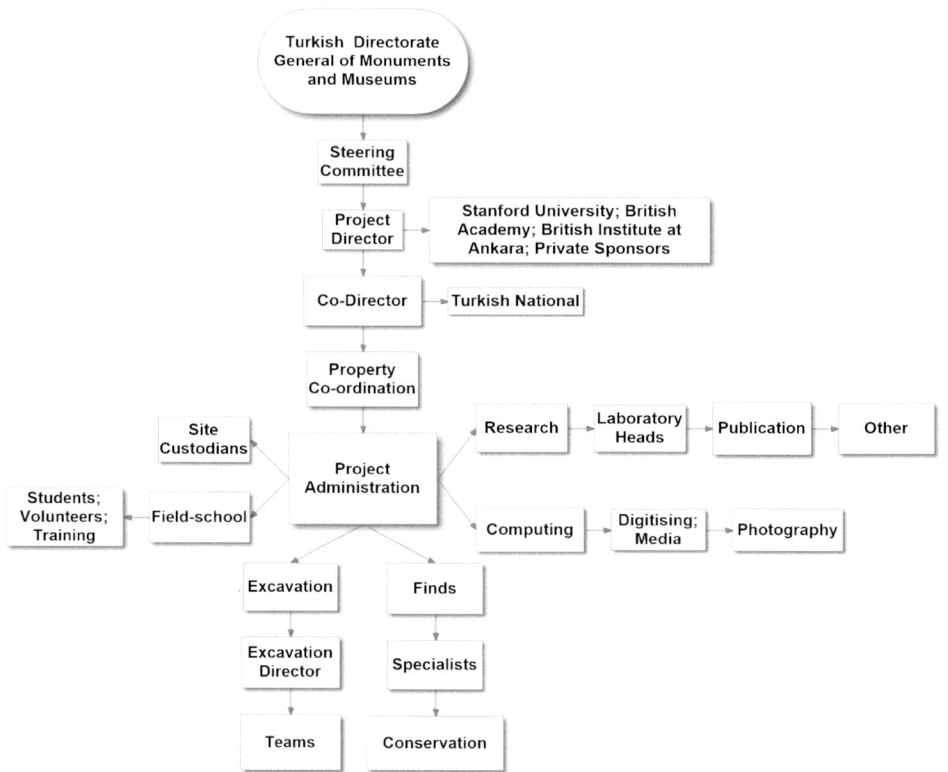

FIGURE 1.10 ORGANISATIONAL STRUCTURE OF ÇATALHÖYÜK IN 2010

Appendix 1: Field Study: Syria and Turkey

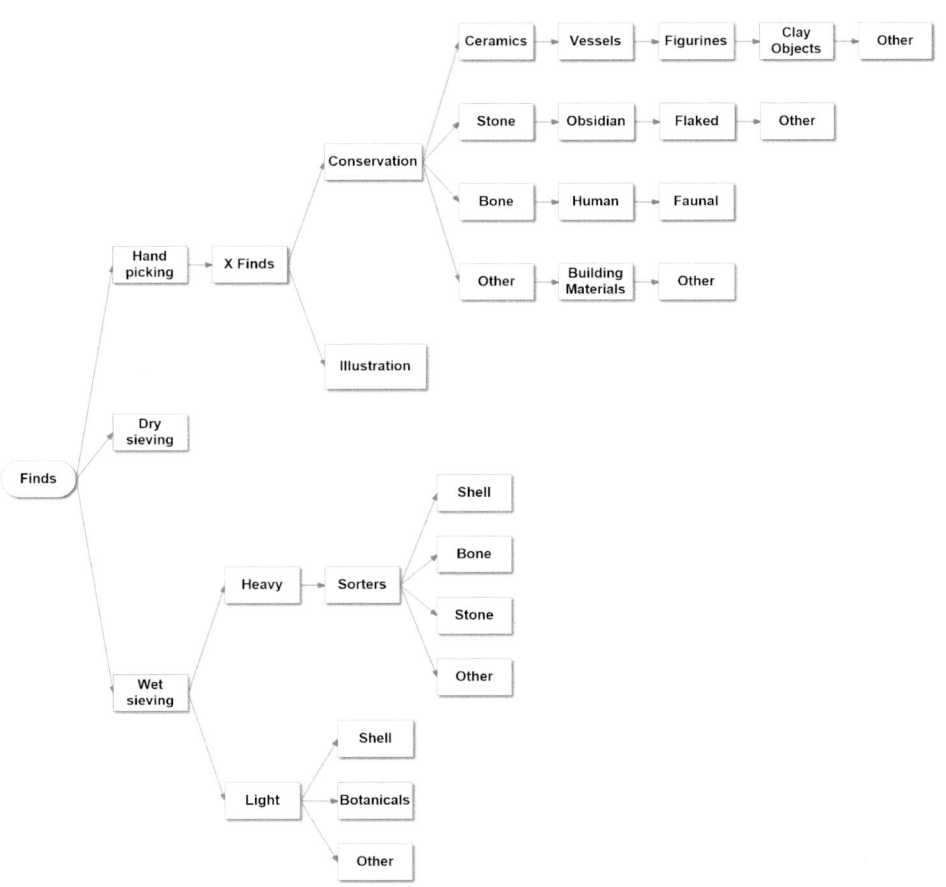

Figure 1.11 Collecting strategy at Çatalhöyük

Research category	Çatalhöyük Specialist Personnel										Total over 9 year period
	2003	2004	2005	2006	2007	2008	2009	2010	2011	2012	
Architectural analysis	-	1	4	2	1	1	1	1	-	-	11
C14 dating and isotopic analysis	-	-	1	1	-	3	2	3	-	-	10
Ceramics and pottery	2	1	4	4	6	3	2	3	4	9	38
Charcoal	-	1	-	-	-	1	-	1	1	1	5
Chipped stone and lithics	3	6	2	4	2	4	3	5	4	11	44
Clay architectural analysis and hearths	-	-	-	-	-	1	1	1	-	2	5
Clay balls and geometric shapes, clay beads	-	2	-	-	-	2	2	2	1	1	10
Clay materiality and sourcing	-	-	-	1	1	1	2	1	1	1	8
Clay stamps	-	1	1	-	-	-	1	-	-	-	3
Ethnoarchaeology, textiles, basketry and social anthropology	7	3	1	-	-	-	1	-	-	-	12
Fauna	6	7	11	12	10	7	7	2	4	13	79
Figurines and miniature clay objects	-	2	2	2	2	2	3	3	4	4	24
Forensics and Chemical analysis	-	-	-	-	-	5	4	2	-	-	1
Ground stone and bead technology	-	1	2	2	5	1	2	5	2	3	23
Heavy residue	2	1	1	2	2	1	2	2	2	1	16
Human remains	3	8	7	10	12	5	12	7	3	13	80
Landscape survey and coring	-	-	-	-	-	4	3	-	-	-	7
Microfauna and micromorphology	-	3	1	3	-	-	3	4	1	4	19
Palaeoethnobotany, phytoliths and starch residue	4	5	8	9	13	11	9	7	7	25	98
Post-chalcolithic assemblage	-	-	-	-	-	-	-	-	2	2	4
Shell	-	-	-	-	-	2	3	2	-	-	7
Speleothem sourcing and sub-surface imaging	-	-	-	-	-	3	2	-	2	2	9
Systems	-	-	-	-	-	-	-	-	-	4	4
Visualisation	-	-	-	-	-	-	5	6	8	8	27

FIGURE 1.12 OVERVIEW OF RESEARCH CATEGORIES AND PARTICIPATING SPECIALISTS FROM 2003 TO 2012

Çatalhöyük Crate Numbers	2010	2012
Douglas Baird survey	365	365
Archaeobot	72	72
Archaeomagnetic	1	1
Architectural samples	5	5
Archive samples	216	249
Brick	5	5
Bead	3	3
Building material	130	129
CBM (Ceramic building material)	20	20
Charcoal	15	16
Chemical analysis samples	1	1
Clay ball	64	69
Clay object	12	16
Core	1	1
Daub	27	27
Eggshell	2	2
Etütlük	16	18
Faunal bone	457	528
Figurines	5	7
Glass and metal	3	4
Ground stone	400	226
Heavy residue	259	119
Human bone	122	161
Kiln library	3	3
Mellaart	21	23
Micromorphology samples	11	11
Natural stone	-	1
Obsidian	26	63
Organic	9	10
Pottery	319	365
Pigment	1	1
Phytolith	22	25
Plaster	23	29
REC/Temper	4	5
Shell	14	17
Surface	-	15
Tile	10	13
Other	18	-
Total	2682	2625

FIGURE 1.13 ÇATALHÖYÜK ARTEFACT CATEGORIES AND CRATE QUANTITIES

Category	Archive samples	Faunal bone	Ground stone	Heavy residue	Human bone	Pottery	Totals
No. crates	249	528	226	119	161	365	1648
% of total	11	23.3	10	5.3	7	16	72.6 %

FIGURE 1.14 QUANTITIES OF CORE ARTEFACT CATEGORIES AND PERCENTAGE OF COLLECTION

Çatalhöyük storage depots	Internal dimensions	Sqm	Maximum capacity (crates)
Unit 1	13.57 m x 6.45 m	87.5	1400
Unit 2	13.58 m x 6.47 m	87.9	1400
Unit 3	10.80 m x 6.44 m	69.6	1100

FIGURE 1.15 ÇATALHÖYÜK STORAGE DEPOT MEASUREMENTS AND CRATE CAPACITIES

No. of crates in storage depots	Total capacity (optimised at 16 crates per m² as at 2012)	Future capacity (optimised at 16 crates per m² as at 2012)	Years left for current facilities (optimised at 16 crates per m² as at 2012)	Years left for current facilities (13.8 crates per m² until 2018)
2414	3900	1486	12.5	8.1

FIGURE 1.16 ESTIMATION OF CAPACITY

Çatalhöyük storage depot construction cost (Central Turkey)	Cost per m²	Annual amortised cost	Total capital requirements for 25-year life of project
USD $45,000 each	$514-$643	$5400	$135,000

FIGURE 1.17 ÇATALHÖYÜK STORAGE DEPOT COST

APPENDIX 1: FIELD STUDY: SYRIA AND TURKEY   97

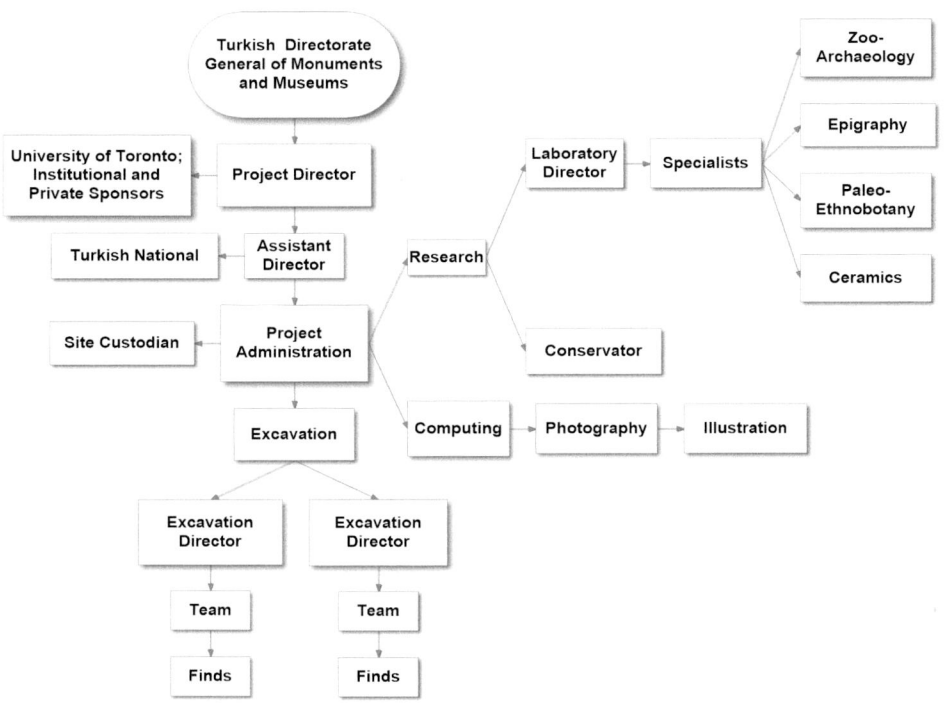

FIGURE 1.18 ORGANISATIONAL STRUCTURE OF TELL TA'YINAT IN 2012

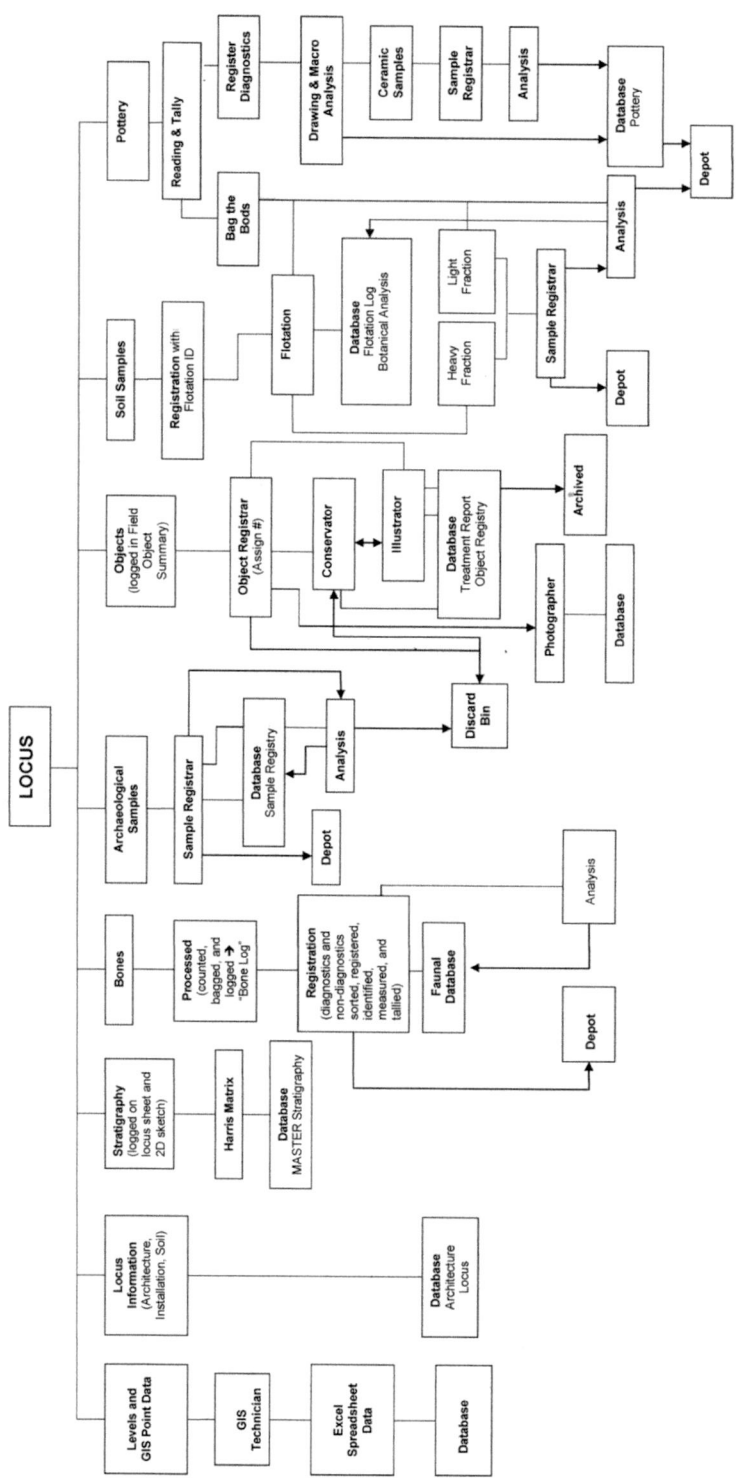

FIGURE 1.19 TELL TA'YINAT 'TRIAGE' SYSTEM

Tell Ta'yinat Field Manual			
	Policy	Processes	Procedures
Pre-Excavation	Locational, Excavation, and Recording Methodologies	Excavation Procedures	Tayinat grid system
			Daily excavation routine
			Mapping
			Locus
			Balks
			Photography
Excavation	Collecting, Conserving, Occupational Health and Safety	Field Artefact Recovery Procedures	Pottery and other clay artefacts
			Glass and faience artefacts
			Plaster and stone or sculptural fragments
			Faunal remains
			Palaeobotanical remains
			Wood and other organic artefacts
			Soil samples
			Radiocarbon samples
Post-Excavation	Processing, Washing, Drying, Registering, Classifying, Analysing	Field Laboratory Procedures	Pottery
			Lithics
			Fauna
			Soil flotation
			Small finds/objects
Documentation	Primary Data Creation	Guidelines for Field Notebooks and Recording Forms	Soil Locus Form
			Architectural Locus Form
			Installation Locus Form
			Burial Supplement Form
			Progress of Excavation Forms
			Macroscopic Ceramic Analysis Form

FIGURE 1.20 POLICIES, PROCESSES AND PROCEDURES IN THE TAP FIELD MANUAL

Crate contents	Pottery body sherds	Pottery diagnostics	Bones	Objects	Miscellaneous (shell, stone, plaster)	Survey	Total
Crates	299	144	34	11	55	3	546
% Total	55	26	6	2	10	<1	100

FIGURE 1.21 TOTAL STORAGE EXPRESSED AS CRATES

TAP operation years (2004–2012)	Total crates per annum	Retractable shelves	Annual kg accumulation
8	68.3	16.2	1024

FIGURE 1.22 TAP ANNUAL CRATE ACCUMULATION

Storage depots	Area	Internal Dimensions	Sqm	Shelving	Crates
No. 1	A	3.0 m x 4.1 m	12	-	56
	B	4.1 m x 4.7 m	25	170	110
No. 2	C	9.3 m x 4.1 m	38	-	608
Total	-	-	75	170	774

FIGURE 1.23 TELL TA'YINAT STORAGE DEPOT MEASUREMENTS AND CRATE CAPACITIES

Storage units	No. of storage units in depots	Total capacity (optimised at 16 crates per m² as at 2012)	Future capacity (optimised at 16 crates per m² as at 2012)	Years left for current facilities (optimised at 16 crates per m² as at 2012)
Crates	481	774	293	4.3
Shelving	130	170	40	2.5

FIGURE 1.24 ESTIMATION OF CAPACITY

Year	No. of accessioned objects
2009–2011	150
2008	42
2007	26
2006	174
Total	392

FIGURE 1.25 NUMBER OF ARTEFACTS ACCESSIONED 2006 TO 2011

APPENDIX 1: FIELD STUDY: SYRIA AND TURKEY

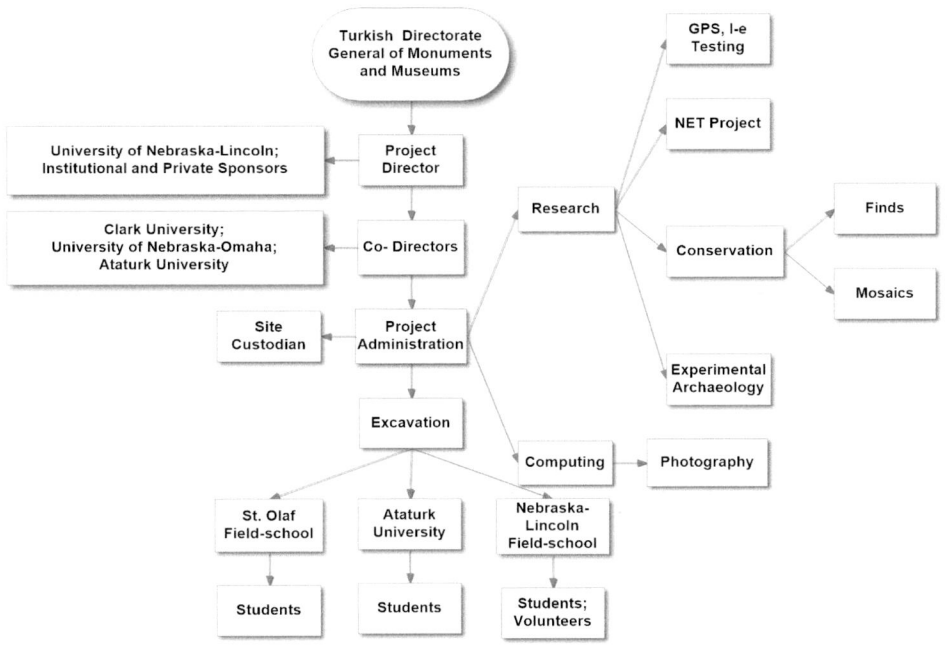

FIGURE 1.26 ORGANISATIONAL STRUCTURE OF ANTIOCHIA AD CRAGUM IN 2013

AACRP Storage Areas 2013	Crates (large: 52 cm x 36 cm x 30 cm)	Crates (small: 49 cm x 35 cm x 20 cm)	Total crates
Dighouse			
Pottery laboratory (temporary)	9	0	9
Total crates (dighouse)	9	0	9
Storage depot (Room 1: 6.95 m x 6.95 m x 2.75 m)			
Unit 1	0	0	0
Unit 2	0	0	0
Unit 3	0	0	0
Unit 4	0	0	
Unit 5	6	0	6
Unit 6	12	4	16
Unit 7	18	1	19
Unit 8	21	0	21
Unit 9	27	2	29
Unit 10	25	5	30
Unit 11	18	3	21
Unit 11 (bagged: crate equivalent)	16	0	16
Unit 12	24	4	28
Unit 12 (on floor beside)	3	0	3
Total crates (Room 1)	179	19	198
Storage depot (Room 2: 4.3 m x 3.0 m x 2.7 5m)			
Total crates (Room 2)	0	0	0
Storage depot (Room 3: 6.95 m x 6.95 m x 2.75 m)			
Total crate equivalent (Room 3)	27	0	27
Total crates stored	206	19	225

FIGURE 1.27 ANTIOCHIA AD CRAGUM ARTEFACT CATEGORIES AND QUANTITIES

Appendix 1: Field Study: Syria and Turkey

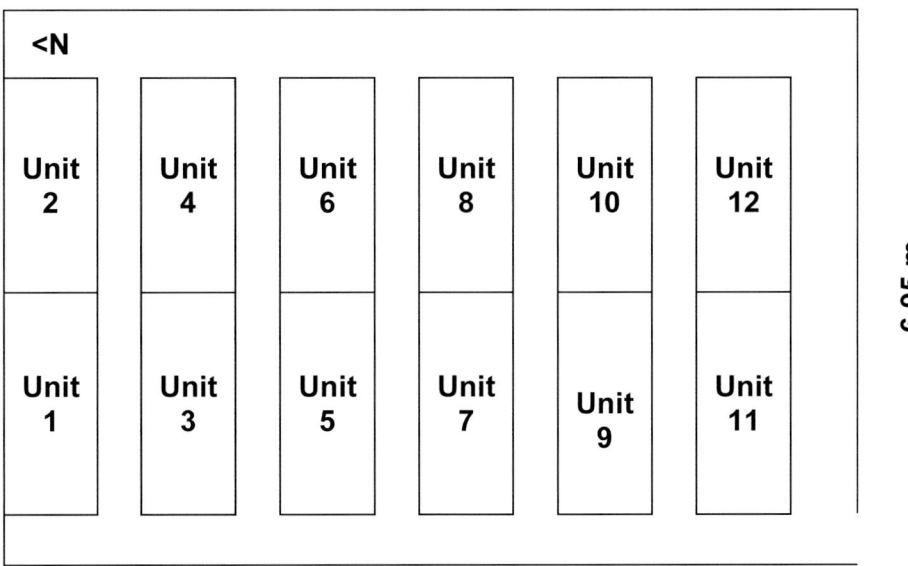

Figure 1.28 Configuration of metal shelving units

Storage areas 2013	Contents description	2009	2010	2011	2012	2013	No date	Total crates
Dighouse	Diagnostic pottery			6	3			9
Storage depot (Room 1)	Main crate storage depot							
Unit 1	Architectural fragments loose on shelves							
Unit 2	Architectural fragments loose on shelves							
Unit 3	Architectural fragments loose on shelves, storage boxes for small finds (coins, painted plaster, metal, bone, lamp fragments, glass)							
Unit 4	Architectural fragments loose on shelves							
Unit 5	Mixed pottery and building materials			4	2			6
Unit 6	Mixed pottery and building materials	4		12				16
Unit 7	Mixed pottery and building materials				19			19
Unit 8	Mixed pottery and building materials				5	16		21
Unit 9	8 pottery; 21 building materials (includes 10 crates from 2013 swimming pool excavation; 4 pottery, 6 building materials)					10	19	29
Unit 10	Mostly building materials, few mixed, (includes 1 pottery crate from 2013 swimming pool excavation)					1	29	30
Unit 11	9 pottery, remainder building materials (includes 9 crates from 2013 swimming pool excavation; 6 pottery, 3 building materials) 8 x 40 kg bags of building materials (roof tile) counted as equivalent to 16 crates x 20kg					9	12	21
							16	16
Unit 12	5 pottery, remainder building materials (includes 6 crates from 2013 swimming pool excavation; 4 pottery, 2 building materials), plus 3 on floor next to unit					9	22	31
(Room 2)	No crates stored	0	0	0	0	0	0	0
(Room 3)	Equipment and temporary pottery and photo laboratories; Total m^3 of space occupied by bags of roof tile (2.3 m x 2.2 m x 0.3 m = 1.5 m^3: divided by 0.056 m^3 (1 crate) volume equivalent to 27 crates; amortised over 2011–2012	0	0	13.5	13.5	0	0	27
Total crates stored		4	0	35.5	42.5	45	98	225

FIGURE 1.29 CRATE ACCUMULATIONS 2009 TO 2012

Appendix 2: Survey: Archaeologists, Conservators and Curators

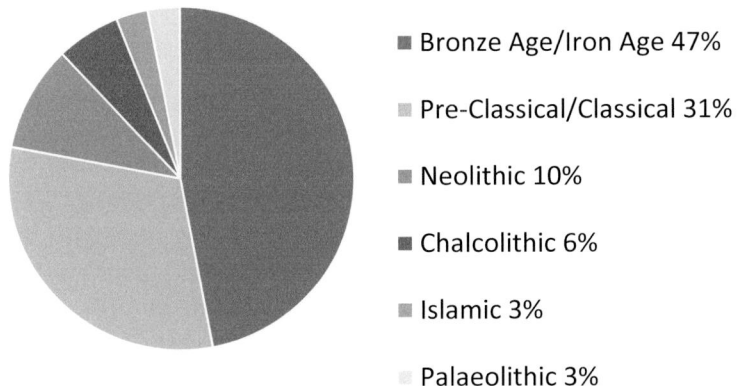

Figure 2.1: Site types directed by survey participants.

Key groups	Survey categories
Archaeologists	Background
	Pre-excavation project design
	Excavation
	Post-excavation
	Opinion
Conservators	Collections
	Excavation
	Quantifying collections
	Opinion
Curators	Collections
	Accession
	Curation
	Quantifying collections
	Research
	Opinion

Figure 2.2: Key groups and survey categories.

Host countries – archaeologists (n = 11)	Afghanistan	Cyprus	Egypt	Greece	Iran	Israel	Jordan	Lebanon	Sicily	Syria	Turkey	Total
Participants	1	1	3	2	2	5	7	1	1	5	4	n=32
Percentage	3	3	9	6	6	16	22	3	3	16	13	100%

FIGURE 2.3: COUNTRIES IN WHICH ARCHAEOLOGISTS WERE WORKING OR HAD WORKED.

Duration of project (years)	1–9	10–19	20–29	30–39	40–59	60–79	80–100+	Total
Participants	8	8	6	4	2	0	2	n=30
Percentage	27	27	19	13	7	0	7	100%

FIGURE 2.4: DURATION OF ARCHAEOLOGICAL PROJECTS.

Duration of directorship (years)	1–9	10–19	20–29	30–49	Total
Participants	12	7	8	3	n=30
Percentage	40	23	27	10	100%

FIGURE 2.5: DURATION OF PROJECT DIRECTORSHIPS.

Managing institution	Government	Private institutions	University institutions	University departments	Total
Participants	3	7	4	16	n=30
Percentage	10	23	14	53	100%

FIGURE 2.6: RELATIONSHIPS OF ARCHAEOLOGICAL PROJECT STAKEHOLDERS.

Duration of funding (years)	1–3	3–5	Mix (1–5)	Ongoing	Expired	Total
Participants	6	7	3	7	1	n=24
Percentage	25	29	13	29	4	100%

FIGURE 2.7: DURATION OF FUNDING FOR ARCHAEOLOGICAL PROJECTS.

Specification of objectives and resources	Yes	No	Total
Participants	27	2	n=29
Percentage	93	7	100%

FIGURE 2.8: SPECIFICATIONS FOR OBJECTIVES AND RESOURCES ARE INCLUDED IN PROJECT DESIGNS.

Specification of aims and costs	Yes	No	Total
Participants	23	3	n=26
Percentage	88	12	100%

FIGURE 2.9: SPECIFICATIONS FOR AIMS AND COSTS ARE INCLUDED IN PROJECT DESIGNS.

Specification of strategies and resources	Yes	No	Total
Participants	22	1	n=23
Percentage	96	4	100%

FIGURE 2.10: SPECIFICATIONS FOR STRATEGIES AND RESOURCES ARE INCLUDED IN PROJECT DESIGNS.

Specifications of assignations	Yes	No	Total
Participants	20	1	n=21
Percentage	95	5	100%

FIGURE 2.11: SPECIFICATIONS FOR ASSIGNATIONS ARE INCLUDED IN PROJECT DESIGNS.

Specification of archive recipient	Yes	No	Total
Participants	20	4	n=24
Percentage	83	17	100%

FIGURE 2.12: SPECIFICATIONS FOR ARCHIVE RECIPIENTS ARE INCLUDED IN PROJECT DESIGNS.

Annual project design update	Yes	No	Total
Participants	22	3	n=25
Percentage	88	12	100%

FIGURE 2.13: ANNUAL UPDATES OF PROJECT DESIGNS ARE PROVIDED.

Pre-excavation management system	Yes	No	Total
Participants	26	3	n=29
Percentage	90	10	100%

FIGURE 2.14: IT SYSTEMS ARE USED FOR PRE-EXCAVATION MANAGEMENT.

On-site management system	Yes	No	Total
Participants	25	6	*n=31*
Percentage	81	19	100%

FIGURE 2.15: IT SYSTEMS ARE USED FOR ON-SITE MANAGEMENT.

Post-excavation management system	Yes	No	Total
Participants	31	0	*n=31*
Percentage	100	0	100%

FIGURE 2.16: IT SYSTEMS ARE USED FOR POST-EXCAVATION MANAGEMENT.

Types of programs and software	Access Database	Excel	Filemaker Pro	Other	Photoshop; Illustrator	Relational Database	Specialised Software	Word
Participants	11	11	6	1	5	3	16	3
Percentage	34	34	19	3	16	9	50	9

FIGURE 2.17: TYPES OF PROGRAMS AND SOFTWARE USED THROUGHOUT PROJECT PHASES.

On-site work	Yes	No	Total
Participants	28	2	*n=30*
Percentage	93	7	100%

FIGURE 2.18: SPECIALISTS IDENTIFY WORK NEEDING TO BE CARRIED OUT ON-SITE.

Timetables and Budgets Responses	Yes	No	Total
Participants	24	5	*n=29*
Percentage	83	17	100%

FIGURE 2.19: TIMETABLES AND BUDGETS ALLOW FOR VISITS BY CONSERVATORS AND SPECIALISTS.

Arrange long-term care	Yes	No	Total
Participants	13	16	*n=29*
Percentage	45	55	100%

FIGURE 2.20: PROJECTS ARRANGE LONG-TERM CARE WITH MUSEUMS IN THE PLANNING STAGE.

Budget long-term care	Yes	No	Total
Participants	12	16	*n=28*
Percentage	43	57	100%

FIGURE 2.21: PROJECTS BUDGET FOR LONG-TERM CARE OF NON-ARTEFACTUAL MATERIAL.

Training manuals	Yes	No	Total
Participants	17	13	*n=30*
Percentage	57	43	100%

FIGURE 2.22: PROJECTS PROVIDE WRITTEN TRAINING MANUALS FOR STUDENTS AND/OR VOLUNTEERS.

In favour of keeping	Yes	No	Total
Participants	16	14	*n=30*
Percentage	53	47	100%

FIGURE 2.23: ARCHAEOLOGISTS ARE IN FAVOUR OF KEEPING A COLLECTION IN PERPETUITY.

Collecting policy	Yes	No	Total
Participants	21	10	*n=31*
Percentage	68	32	100%

FIGURE 2.24: PROJECTS SPECIFY AN ARTEFACT COLLECTING POLICY.

Sampling policy	Yes	No	Total
Participants	18	12	*n=30*
Percentage	60	40	100%

FIGURE 2.25: PROJECTS SPECIFY AN ARTEFACT SAMPLING POLICY.

Discard policy	Yes	No	Don't discard	Total
Participants	14	14	3	*n=31*
Percentage	45	45	10	100%

FIGURE 2.26: PROJECTS SPECIFY AN ARTEFACT DISCARD POLICY.

Redundancy policy	Yes	No	Total
Participants	9	20	*n=29*
Percentage	31	69	100%

FIGURE 2.27: PROJECTS SPECIFY A SAMPLING STRATEGY FOR REDUNDANT OBJECTS.

Archaeologists	Most to least 'useful' rating
Context	1
Site significance	2
Datability	3
Diversity, rarity	4
Condition	5

FIGURE 2.28: ARCHAEOLOGISTS' RATING OF SIGNIFICANCE CRITERIA IN ORDER OF MOST TO LEAST USEFUL.

Responses	Yes	No	Total
Participants	28	0	n=28
Percentage	100	0	100%

FIGURE 2.29: PROJECTS BRIEF RELEVANT CONSULTANTS ON DATA COLLECTION POLICIES.

Responses	Yes	No	Total
Participants	29	0	n=29
Percentage	100	0	100%

FIGURE 2.30: PROJECTS EXPLAIN ON-SITE PROCEDURES TO EXCAVATORS.

Responses	Yes	No	Total
Participants	27	2	n=29
Percentage	93	7	100%

FIGURE 2.31: PROJECTS UNDERTAKE INDIVIDUAL TRAINING.

Responses	Yes	No	Total
Participants	23	5	n=28
Percentage	82	12	100%

FIGURE 2.32: PROJECTS HAVE A SYSTEM FOR DETECTING ERRORS MADE DURING FIELDWORK.

Primary Data Archive	% of archaeologists
Context records	85
Maps, plans, sections	85
Photographic records	77
Datasets for artefacts and samples	73
Finds records, registers, catalogues, inventories	65
Field notebooks, diaries	62
Other	54
Computer discs and print-outs	50
Survey records, GIS	27
Samples records	19
Skeleton records	12
Conservation records, x-ray records	8

FIGURE 2.33: DOCUMENTS AND RECORDS COMPRISING THE PRIMARY DATA ARCHIVE.

Categories	1	2	3	4	5	
Responses	0–999	1000–4999	5000–9999	10000–19999	20000+	Total
Participants	7	9	3	1	1	n=21
Percentage	33	43	14	5	5	100

FIGURE 2.34: NUMBERS OF INVENTORIED (REGISTERED) OBJECTS PER SEASON.

Appendix 2: Survey: Archaeologists, Conservators and Curators

Responses	1–25%	26–50%	51–75%	76–100%	Total
Participants	8	1	0	8	n=17
Percentage	47	6	0	47	100%

Figure 2.35: Percentage of inventoried objects accessioned by museums.

Responses	Specific Nos.	Approximate Nos.	Total
Participants	6	13	n=19
Percentage	32	68	100%

Figure 2.36: Approximate numbers of objects requiring conservation.

Responses	Yes	No	Total
Participants	15	13	n=28
Percentage	53	47	100

Figure 2.37: Written notification of conservation treatments is provided.

Responses	Yes	No	Total
Participants	8	20	n=28
Percentage	28	72	100%

Figure 2.38: Written notification of further conservation work required is provided.

Responses	Specific amounts	Approximations	No idea; don't know	Total
Participants	9	4	4	n=17
Percentage	52	24	24	100%

Figure 2.39: Approximate (kg) amount of excavated material each season.

Responses	Yes	No	Total
Participants	26	5	n=31
Percentage	84	16	100%

Figure 2.40: Archaeological projects have storage facilities on-site or nearby.

Responses	Short-term only	Short- and long-term	Unsure how long	Total
Participants	5	13	4	n=22
Percentage	23	59	18	100%
Short-term = less than 5 years; long-term = 5 to 20+ years				

Figure 2.41: Duration of adequacy and availability of storage space.

Responses	Specific amounts	Approximations	Total
Participants	8	11	n=19
Percentage	42	58	100%

FIGURE 2.42: TOTAL SPACE (M3) OCCUPIED BY ARTEFACTS AND COLLECTIONS.

Responses	Yes	No	Total
Participants	23	6	n=29
Percentage	79	21	100%

FIGURE 2.43: ARCHAEOLOGISTS ACCESS ARCHAEOLOGICAL COLLECTIONS FOR RESEARCH.

Responses	Yes	No	Total
Participants	16	7	n=23
Percentage	70	30	100%

FIGURE 2.44: ARTEFACTS AND COLLECTIONS ARE EASILY ACCESSIBLE.

Responses	Yes	No	Total
Participants	14	8	n=22
Percentage	64	36	100%

FIGURE 2.45: ARTEFACTS AND COLLECTIONS ARE IN GOOD CONDITION.

Responses	Yes	No	Total
Participants	13	10	n=23
Percentage	56	44	100%

FIGURE 2.46: ARTEFACTS AND COLLECTIONS HAVE AN ACCOMPANYING ARCHIVE.

Host countries – conservators (n = 7)	Egypt	Greece	Iran	Israel	Jordan	Lebanon	Turkey	Total
Participants	3	2	1	1	2	1	2	n=12
Percentage	25	17	8	8	17	8	17	100%

FIGURE 2.47: COUNTRIES IN WHICH CONSERVATORS WORKED OR HAD WORKED.

APPENDIX 2: SURVEY: ARCHAEOLOGISTS, CONSERVATORS AND CURATORS

Conservators	Most to least 'useful' rating
Rarity	1
Context	2
Datability	3
Condition	4
Diversity	5
Site significance	6

FIGURE 2.48: CONSERVATORS' RATING OF SIGNIFICANCE CRITERIA IN ORDER OF MOST TO LEAST USEFUL.

Responses	Yes	No	Other explanation	Total
Participants	7	0	1	n=8
Percentage	78	0	22	100%

FIGURE 2.49: CONSERVATORS GIVE ADVICE ABOUT CONSERVATION INTERVENTIONS PERFORMED.

Responses	Yes	Other explanation	Total
Participants	8	1	n=9
Percentage	89	11	100%

FIGURE 2.50: CONSERVATORS GIVE ADVICE FOR LONG-TERM CARE OF OBJECTS/COLLECTIONS.

Responses	Yes	No	Total
Participants	10	1	n=11
Percentage	91	9	100%

FIGURE 2.51: CONSERVATORS ARE SATISFIED WITH ON-SITE RESOURCES.

Responses	Yes	No	Total
Participants	9	2	n=11
Percentage	82	18	100%

FIGURE 2.52: CONSERVATORS ARE TRAINED IN ARCHAEOLOGICAL EXCAVATION TECHNIQUES.

Responses	Yes	No	Other explanation	Total
Participants	1	5	3	n=9
Percentage	11	56	33	100%

FIGURE 2.53: CONSERVATORS BELIEVE ARCHAEOLOGISTS HAVE A GOOD UNDERSTANDING OF CONSERVATION.

Host countries – curators (n=7)	Australia	Cyprus	Jordan	Lebanon	UAE	UK	USA	Total
Participants	2	2	1	1	2	1	7	n=16
Percentage	13	13	6	6	13	6	43	100%

FIGURE 2.54: COUNTRIES IN WHICH CURATORS WORKED OR HAD WORKED.

Curators	Most to least 'useful' rating
Context	1
Site significance	2
Rarity	3
Datability	4
Diversity	5
Condition	6

FIGURE 2.55: CURATORS' RATING OF SIGNIFICANCE CRITERIA IN ORDER OF MOST TO LEAST USEFUL.

Responses	Yes	No	Total
Participants	15	0	n=15
Percentage	100	0	100%

FIGURE 2.56: ARCHAEOLOGICAL COLLECTIONS ARE HELD IN MUSEUMS/REPOSITORIES.

Responses	Yes	No	Other explanation	Total
Participants	3	9	3	n=15
Percentage	20	60	20	100%

FIGURE 2.57: MUSEUMS/REPOSITORIES HAVE WRITTEN GUIDELINES FOR PACKING ARTEFACTS AND COLLECTIONS.

Responses	Yes	No	Other explanation	Total
Participants	1	7	2	n=10
Percentage	10	70	20	100%

FIGURE 2.58: MUSEUMS/REPOSITORIES SPECIFY EXPECTATIONS UPON DELIVERY OF ARTEFACTS/COLLECTIONS.

Responses	Yes	No	Total
Participants	4	12	n=16
Percentage	27	73	100%

FIGURE 2.59: MUSEUMS/REPOSITORIES REQUEST OBJECTS IN A STABILISED AND/OR CONSERVED CONDITION.

Appendix 2: Survey: Archaeologists, Conservators and Curators

Responses	Yes	No	Total
Participants	2	11	*n=13*
Percentage	15	85	100%

Figure 2.60: Museums/repositories receive advice detailing conservation treatments needed.

Responses	Yes	No	Other explanation	Total
Participants	3	8	4	*n=15*
Percentage	20	53	27	100%

Figure 2.61: Museums/repositories have a curation agreement.

Responses	Yes	No	Other explanation	Total
Participants	3	5	3	*n=11*
Percentage	27	46	27	100%

Figure 2.62: Museums/repositories receive advice detailing long-term plans for collections.

Responses	Yes	No	Other explanation	Total
Participants	6	8	1	*n=15*
Percentage	40	53	7	100%

Figure 2.63: Museums/repositories are involved in the excavation process.

Responses	Yes	No	Other explanation	Total
Participants	4	1	4	*n=9*
Percentage	44	12	44	100%

Figure 2.64: Museums/repositories specify ownership of artefacts/collections.